The Southern Vegetable Book

The Southern Vegetable Book

A ROOT-TO-STALK GUIDE
TO THE SOUTH'S FAVORITE PRODUCE

BY REBECCA LANG

Oxmoor House®

©2016 Time Inc. Books
Published by Oxmoor House, an imprint of Time Inc. Books
225 Liberty Street, 4th Floor, New York, NY 10281

Southern Living is a registered trademark of Time Inc. Lifestyle Group.

Senior Editors: Katherine Cobbs, Rachel Quinlivan West, R.D.
Assistant Project Editors: Melissa Brown, Lauren Moriarty
Senior Designers: Melissa Clark, Maribeth Jones
Cover and Letter Artist: Michael Tabie, Two Arms Inc.
Executive Photography Director: Iain Bagwell
Photo Editor: Kellie Lindsey
Photographers: Hélène Dujardin, Victor Protasio
Senior Photo Stylists: Kay E. Clarke, Mindi Shapiro Levine
Food Stylists: Nathan Carrabba, Victoria E. Cox, Margaret Monroe Dickey,
  Catherine Crowell Steele
Food Styling Assistant: Rishon Hanners
Test Kitchen Manager: Alyson Moreland Haynes
Senior Recipe Developer and Tester: Callie Nash
Recipe Developers and Testers: Julia Levy, Karen Rankin
Assistant Production Director: Sue Chodakiewicz
Assistant Production Manager: Diane Rose Keener
Copy Editors: Donna Baldone, Julie Bosché
Proofreader: Julie Gillis
Indexer: Nanette Cardon
Fellows: Jessica Baude, Dree Deacon, Olivia Pierce, Natalie Schumann, Mallory Short

ISBN-13: 978-0-8487-4688-9
ISBN-10: 0-8487-4688-0
Library of Congress Control Number: 2015954515

Printed in China
10 9 8 7 6 5 4 3 2 1
First Printing 2016

For Kevin, Camden, and Adair
The three of you are my home.

from the author

I was a lucky child. Vegetables seemed to be everywhere. If there weren't plump tomatoes on the vine, there were mustard greens swishing in the sink or huge Vidalia onions being carefully loaded into the legs of pantyhose. I may not have been very high off the ground when I started to take note of the vegetables in my life, but I still was drawn in by their vivid colors, range of aromas, and the way they seemed to bring everyone together.

Thanks to growing up in a farming community, I often saw vegetables come in the back door in bushels rather than in grocery store bags. It was those grand volumes of fresh produce that drew my parents and my grandmothers to the screened porch to shuck, shell, string, or snap. Fingers would work while legs gently nudged gliders and rockers into a contagious rhythm. My hometown was small but the crops seemed to be plentiful. It was a town surrounded by farmland and pine trees. It was an ideal setting to learn the value of the journey from seed to plate.

The South has been home to some of America's most fertile soil for generations. We take pride in the harvest and pay homage to each season by what's cooked in our kitchens. The long Southern growing season makes farmers from most other regions envious.

Our relationship with the vegetables we eat is ever changing. We've gone from a time when vegetables were planted, nurtured, and harvested only by those who would eat them to a day when nearly every vegetable is available year-round in the produce section. A new respect for vegetables is emerging as we Southerners recommit to the standards that our grandparents lived and farmed by. Eat what's in season, put up for when it's not, cook what grows nearby, and be thankful for the Southern soil, the rain, and the sun.

—Rebecca Lang

Introduction to Southern Vegetables

Thanks to farmers' markets and local sources,
we now realize what our grandparents knew all along and pay
respect to all the glorious produce the Southern soil offers.

We live in a time where many family farms surrounding our towns have been turned into subdivisions, and congested interstates equal longer and longer commutes between plant and plate. After years of this belief that seasonless eating was better, we are finally coming to our senses and eating closer to home in the season that each vegetable was intended to be consumed. Our grandparents knew this. Our great-great grandparents knew this. Over the years, we seemed to have lost our way, but we are, at last, seeing clearer.

Tomatoes taste better in summer for a reason. Asparagus in springtime is sweeter. Not only do vegetables explode with more flavor when harvested in their God-given season, but their appearance serves as marks on a natural calendar to remind us what should be on our plates.

Because seasons overlap in the South, many vegetables can grow in both spring and fall. That's one beauty of having growing seasons that gently flow one into another with rarely a single jolt of change. Beets may appear on your Thanksgiving table as well as your Easter table. Carrots are likely to do the same. It's one of the perks of living in the South.

Start a weekly vegetable plate tradition for supper at least one day a week. You'll be shocked at the money you'll save and appreciate the vitamin and antioxidant punch you're adding to your diet. Keep an eye on the colors on your plate. You want to enjoy the greatest mix of vegetables all across the spectrum of colors. From deep red beets to snow white cauliflower, each and every color is nutritionally valuable.

WAYS TO SHOP FOR THE BEST VEGETABLES

Shopping for vegetables today means you have a plethora of choices. Grocery stores appear every mile in some cities and farmers' markets are popping up more and more. Some farmers offer shares in their farms in what is called community supported agriculture, which provides a range of produce that varies week to week in exchange for your investment. With so many options and such a difference between them all, it can be hard to decipher what the best source is. Here are my tips for buying the best vegetables no matter where you shop.

GROCERY STORES

In the grocery store, make sure to read labels of country of origins of vegetables and the information on any that are labeled organic. If a pint of blueberries came all the way from Chile, you need to know that. Even in the grocery store, I try to buy what's in season. I wouldn't buy a watermelon in December (although I could). Be your own advocate. Slow down and read what you're eating.

FARMERS' MARKETS

Farmers' markets are the most accessible source for most people to get the freshest vegetables possible. In some places, they are held year-round, while other markets are only seasonal. The beauty is that you can talk with the farmers and ask questions about the vegetables and how they're grown—or even get their tips for how to cook them. Knowing the person who grows your food is a blessing for both the customer and the farmer. You can touch the vegetables before you buy and purchase only the amount that you need. Plus, there tends to be less waste when shopping close to the source.

COMMUNITY SUPPORTED AGRICULTURE (CSA)

In a CSA, the farmer sells "shares" of that season's crops to customers in exchange for a weekly box of vegetables. The types of vegetables included change over the course of the season and often feature some unexpected additions like kohlrabi and Romanesco cauliflower, which makes cooking them interesting. CSAs help the farmers because they are paid before harvest time, which helps them determine how much of a crop they will need to grow in order to fill the orders. I belong to a CSA and my produce is normally harvested the same day I bring home the box. The freshness is incredible.

VEGETABLE STORAGE

Storing what you buy or grow is as important as knowing how to pick produce that's perfectly ripe. There are tricks for keeping the ideal tomato for a few hours and for freezing the season's finest. Here are the best vegetable storage tips that I've learned over the years:

- Don't wash any vegetable until right before you're going to use it. Excess water speeds deterioration and usually takes away from the texture. Soil on vegetables really does serve a purpose. It often keeps the vegetable fresher longer.
- For vegetables that like to hang out at room temperature, give them space for air to circulate around them. Avoid direct sunlight shining on any countertop produce. An old-fashioned (but still very effective) way to store Vidalia onions at room temperature is to load them into the legs of clean pantyhose. The hose are twisted between each onion so the onions have airflow but don't touch each other.

- The freezer can be your ally as long as you seal out the air from the vegetables. I like to freeze in small batches so I can pull out two cups of tomatoes or lady peas at a time for an impromptu addition to dinner. Zip-top plastic freezer bags are my containers of choice. I like to write the freezing date on each bag before placing it in the freezer.
- For chilling in the refrigerator, do not ever store vegetables in an airtight container. Sealing in air for a fresh vegetable hastens deterioration, so use open plastic and paper bags instead.
- If a vegetable has a green leafy top, like carrots or beets, remove the top before storing the edible roots. The leaves will continue to take nutrients and moisture from the root until they are removed. Store the leaves and roots separately so you can enjoy both of them at their freshest.

MAKING THE RIGHT VEGETABLE CUT

Cutting vegetables is often the first step to cooking or even just serving them raw on the plate. It's important to keep your knives sharp and never let your attention drop from the vegetable that you're chopping, slicing, or cutting. I have my knives professionally sharpened about every nine months at my favorite cookware shop. If a straight-edged knife needs a sawing action to work well, it probably needs sharpening.

- For simple slices like tomatoes for sandwiches, I use a tomato knife. It's a serrated knife that also has a forked tip perfect for picking up the slice and adding it to the bread. The blade is normally about 5 inches long and is the ideal size for any soft vegetable that's easily crushed with a straight-edged knife.
- For larger, tougher slicing, like butternut squash or sweet potatoes, cut an edge to make it flat. It's very easy to cut yourself when you're working with a rolling vegetable and a knife. Stabilizing the vegetable first with a flat edge to rest on makes it safer and much less frustrating for the cook.
- For greens, I like to fold over the leaves, as I would a taco shell, and cut out the stem from the center. Plus, larger leaves are much easier to slice if rolled or folded over so you can cut both sides of the leaves together at the same time.

SHUCKING, SHELLING, AND SNAPPING ON THE PORCH

Families that used to meet on porches to shell peas, shuck corn, and string beans are becoming a thing of the past. With more farmers being equipped with machines that shell and clean vegetables, a gathering for shelling is less common than it used to be. It's also less likely that families today are buying vegetables in a large quantity that requires a lot of prep for storage, or "putting up," just to preserve it. Don't let that go by the wayside. Even if your family is far away, invite friends and neighbors and do what Southerners do. Congregating on the porch with a small mountain of fresh vegetables instantly creates a sense of community and common ground.

Spring

Spring vegetables are those that shine on their own,
with no need for fancy additions. Just like the season, they are tender,
simple, joyous, and delicious straight from the source.

Asparagus

This long slender stalk is a user-friendly vegetable in the kitchen and a test of patience for a gardener. Planting a bed of asparagus often doesn't offer any benefits to the gardener for at least four years.

The stalks come in a range of sizes to meet a cook's preferences. Unlike most vegetables, asparagus keeps growing even after it's picked. If at all possible, look for a farmer's stand at the market that has cut their spears below the surface of the ground. The bottom of the stalks will be nearly white. This technique helps the stalks retain moisture and keeps them fresher longer. Use the asparagus as soon as possible after picking or buying. The natural sugars begin to decline moments after harvest. If a recipe doesn't call for a specific size, simply choose your liking. They can range greatly from the width of a pencil to that of a marker.

Store the stalks upright in a container with a little water, like you would a bouquet of flowers, for up to two days. Cut off the tough ends before cooking but save them for adding asparagus flavor to homemade stock for soups and stews.

WHITE BEAN-AND-ASPARAGUS SALAD

This stir-together, make-ahead salad is practically made for covered dish gatherings. The cannellini beans, dried tomatoes, and fresh asparagus are a colorful combination on top of salad greens.

MAKES 6 SERVINGS   HANDS-ON 20 MINUTES   TOTAL 1 HOUR, 24 MINUTES

½ lb. fresh asparagus, trimmed

7 dried tomatoes

1 garlic clove, minced

1 Tbsp. brown sugar

2 Tbsp. extra virgin olive oil

2 Tbsp. white wine vinegar

1 tsp. spicy brown mustard

¼ tsp. dried rubbed sage

¼ tsp. table salt

¼ tsp. freshly ground black pepper

1 (19-oz.) can cannellini beans, drained and rinsed

¼ cup chopped red onion

2 tsp. drained capers

1 (5-oz.) bag gourmet mixed salad greens

1 Tbsp. shredded Parmesan cheese

1. Arrange asparagus and dried tomatoes in a steamer basket over boiling water. Cover and steam 2 to 4 minutes or until asparagus is crisp-tender. Set tomatoes aside. Plunge asparagus into ice water to stop the cooking process; drain. Cut asparagus into 1-inch pieces, and chill until ready to use. Chop tomatoes.

2. Whisk together garlic, next 7 ingredients, and 1 tablespoon water in a medium bowl; add asparagus, tomatoes, beans, onion, and capers, tossing to coat. Cover and chill 1 hour. Serve asparagus mixture over salad greens; sprinkle with cheese.

FETTUCCINE-AND-ASPARAGUS AL BURRO

I love pasta that's easy enough for a weeknight supper but pretty enough for company. This classic combination of pancetta and asparagus is dressed with a luxurious butter sauce, or *al burro* in Italian. Buy authentic Parmigiano-Reggiano, and you'll be glad you did.

MAKES 3 TO 4 SERVINGS   HANDS-ON 30 MINUTES   TOTAL 30 MINUTES

1 lb. fresh thin asparagus

4 to 6 oz. thick pancetta slices, diced

1 (9-oz.) package refrigerated fettuccine

2 Tbsp. butter, at room temperature

3 Tbsp. extra virgin olive oil

½ cup freshly shredded Parmigiano-Reggiano cheese

2 Tbsp. chopped fresh flat-leaf parsley

¼ tsp. table salt

¼ tsp. freshly ground black pepper

Toppings: shredded Parmigiano-Reggiano cheese, freshly ground black pepper

1. Snap off and discard tough ends of asparagus. Cut asparagus diagonally into 1½-inch pieces.

2. Sauté pancetta in a large skillet over medium heat 5 minutes or until crisp; remove from skillet.

3. Cook fettuccine and asparagus in boiling salted water to cover 2 to 3 minutes. Drain, reserving ¼ cup pasta water.

4. Melt butter with oil in skillet over medium heat; add hot cooked pasta and asparagus, cheese, and next 3 ingredients. Toss to coat, adding enough reserved pasta water to make a glossy sauce. Remove from heat; sprinkle with pancetta. Serve immediately with desired toppings.

ASPARAGUS WITH ROSEMARY AÏOLI

I learned as a child, right or wrong, that it was acceptable to eat asparagus by picking it up like a French fry. So I've always been a fan of dipping the spears into sauces for fun—good manners or not. Thicker asparagus is best for this recipe, so look for the fattest spears. The tips will be toasty browned and crispy after roasting.

MAKES 4 TO 6 SERVINGS   HANDS-ON 10 MINUTES   TOTAL 45 MINUTES

3 lb. fresh asparagus

2 Tbsp. extra virgin olive oil

½ tsp. table salt

¼ tsp. freshly ground black pepper

½ cup mayonnaise

2 garlic cloves, minced

1 Tbsp. finely chopped fresh rosemary

1 Tbsp. fresh lemon juice

Garnish: fresh rosemary

1. Preheat oven to 450°F. Snap off and discard tough ends of asparagus. Toss with olive oil. Arrange in a single layer on a jelly-roll pan. Sprinkle with salt and pepper.

2. Roast at 450°F for 35 to 40 minutes or until browned and crispy. (Asparagus will look shriveled.)

3. To make aïoli, combine mayonnaise, garlic, rosemary, and lemon juice. Serve asparagus with aïoli for dipping.

✦ sage advice ✦

Vegetables intended for dinner should be gathered early in the morning. Only a few can be kept 12 hours without detriment.
—Annabella P. Hill in
Mrs. Hill's Southern Practical Cookery and Receipt Book (1872)

Beets

Beets are originally from the Mediterranean and are known for their intense red coloring, their earthy taste, and a touch of sweetness. Thanks to farmers who have brought back heirloom varieties to the delight of beet fans everywhere, the range of colors now varies far from the crimson spectrum.

Look for beets with greens that are bright and crisp. In general, small and medium beets are more tender than larger ones. The delightfully salty beet greens are great in a salad or sautéed as a side. Peeling beets can be quite the chore with a vegetable peeler.

Now, I like to steam the beets in their skins in foil packets until they're done. Simply wrap beets in heavy-duty aluminum foil and make sure to seal the edges so the steam and heat won't escape. Bake at 400°F for about an hour and a half or until tender. Remarkably, the skins will then slip off much like a banana peel.

To store, remove the greens and keep beets wrapped in a damp towel in the refrigerator for up to five days.

BEET-POPPY SEED MUFFINS

Beets are shredded for these sweet and citrusy muffins. The effect is a beautiful hue of pink with no artificial coloring. The natural moisture in the beets eliminates the dreaded dry muffin.

MAKES 12 SERVINGS   HANDS-ON 15 MINUTES   TOTAL 35 MINUTES

1½ cups all-purpose flour

¾ cup firmly packed dark brown sugar

1 Tbsp. poppy seeds

1¼ tsp. baking powder

½ tsp. baking soda

½ tsp. table salt

2 large eggs

5 Tbsp. olive oil

1 Tbsp. firmly packed orange zest

1 large fresh beet, peeled and shredded (about 1½ cups)

12 paper baking cups

Vegetable cooking spray

1. Preheat oven to 375°F. Whisk together flour, brown sugar, poppy seeds, baking powder, baking soda, and salt in a large bowl. Stir in eggs, olive oil, and orange zest. Fold in shredded beet. (Do not squeeze juice from shredded beet.)

2. Place paper baking cups in a 12-cup muffin pan. Coat cups with cooking spray. Spoon batter into cups, filling two-thirds full. Bake at 375°F for 20 to 22 minutes or until golden brown.

sage advice

Try the green tops of vegetables like beets and turnips sautéed with olive oil and butter. Thinly slice them for easy handling, and cook until wilted. Raw beet greens, with a kale-like taste, are great mixed with lettuce or spinach in a salad.

LEMONY BEET DIP

My family loves beets in red, yellow, pink, and any other color we can get our hands on. This bright red spread is a favorite of ours on pita chips and sliced celery. It's a refreshing change, in color and taste, from standard hummus. Try it with spinach and sweet onions on a tortilla for a colorful wrap for lunch.

MAKES ABOUT 2 CUPS   HANDS-ON 15 MINUTES   TOTAL 2 HOURS

2 lb. beets with green tops

1 garlic clove

¾ cup pecan halves

½ cup extra virgin olive oil

Zest of 1 lemon (about 2 tsp.)

¼ cup fresh lemon juice

½ tsp. table salt

⅓ cup finely crumbled feta cheese

Garnish: chopped fresh chives

Crackers or crostini

1. Preheat oven to 400°F. Remove tops from beets, reserve for another use. (Refer to page 26.) Wrap beets in heavy-duty aluminum foil, making sure to seal completely into a packet so steam can't escape. Roast at 400°F for 1 hour and 45 minutes or until soft. Cool to room temperature and slip off peeling. Cut beets into fourths.

2. Pulse garlic in a food processor until finely minced. Add pecans; pulse to finely chop. Add beets; pulse. Add olive oil and next 3 ingredients; process until smooth.

3. Transfer to a serving bowl or shallow dish. Top with ⅓ cup finely crumbled feta. Serve with crackers or crostini.

PICKLED PINK DEVILED EGGS

Dressing up deviled eggs with a pink hue is both fun and unexpected. The natural dye from beets is perfect for the job. Watch the clock for soaking the eggs. If they sit longer, they will have a bit of a pickled flavor. Yellow and orange beets work just as well and are equally exciting to try! Older eggs are best for peeling, so try to remember to do your shopping several days in advance, if possible.

MAKES 2 DOZEN   HANDS-ON 30 MINUTES   TOTAL 4 HOURS

12 large eggs

⅓ cup white wine vinegar

⅓ cup apple cider vinegar

2 red beets, peeled and cut in half

1 Tbsp. sugar

2½ tsp. table salt, divided

⅓ cup mayonnaise

1 Tbsp. chopped fresh chives

1½ tsp. Dijon mustard

¼ tsp. freshly ground black pepper

Garnish: chopped fresh chives

1. Bring 2 inches of water to a boil in a large Dutch oven. Add eggs. Boil for 10 minutes. Transfer eggs to ice water to sit for 5 minutes. Crack and peel.

2. Bring vinegars, beets, sugar, 2 teaspoons salt, and 4 cups water to a boil. Remove from heat; cool.

3. In a nonreactive bowl, cover peeled eggs with beet mixture. Eggs should be submerged. Cover and chill for 3 hours.

4. Remove eggs from beet liquid and dry on a paper towel-lined plate. Slice eggs in half lengthwise, and carefully remove yolks, keeping egg whites intact. Grate egg yolks using small holes of a box grater. Mash together yolks, remaining ½ teaspoon salt, mayonnaise, and next 3 ingredients. Spoon or pipe yolk mixture into egg whites.

Carrots

Carrots didn't start out orange. They were first cultivated in the Middle East as purple vegetables, but orange eventually took over as the preferred color after their popularity rose in the Netherlands. Now as heirloom seeds are prevailing, rainbow carrots have become quite common in farmers' markets. The skins do contain nutrients, which give you a great excuse to skip peeling them.

Look for firm carrots with lush tops. Larger carrots are sweeter, thanks to the sugars being stored on the outer layers (away from the core). The tops can be bitter, but chopping a small amount and using them for garnish can be a beautiful burst of color.

Remove the tops and store the roots in an open bag for up to five days.

CARROT-APPLE SOUP

The sweetness of carrots and the tartness of apples combine to make magic in this very simple soup. Simmering in just one pot before blending is a cook's dream. The color is as bright as just-picked carrots.

MAKES 7 CUPS   HANDS-ON 30 MINUTES   TOTAL 1 HOUR, 45 MINUTES

1½ lb. carrots, peeled and chopped (about 8 large)

3 tart apples (such as Granny Smith) or creamy apples (such as McIntosh), peeled and chopped (about 1 lb.)

1 large yellow onion, chopped

2 cups heavy cream

1½ cups unsalted chicken stock

1¼ cups apple cider

3 fresh thyme sprigs

1 tsp. kosher salt

½ tsp. freshly ground black pepper

Garnishes: sour cream, diced apples, thyme sprigs

1. Bring all ingredients except garnishes to a boil in a Dutch oven over medium-high heat; reduce heat to low, and simmer, stirring occasionally, 50 to 60 minutes or until carrots are tender. Remove from heat, and cool 15 minutes.

2. Remove thyme sprigs. Process soup, in batches, in a blender or food processor until smooth. (For a thinner soup, stir in more broth, 1 tablespoon at a time.) Spoon into individual bowls, and serve immediately.

put 'em up

One way to use an excess of fresh vegetables is to make your own homemade vegetable broth. There's a world of difference in homemade broth and what you can buy at the grocery store. Here's a basic recipe you can make to keep on hand: Combine 3 cups chopped onion, 2 cups chopped carrot, 2 cups chopped celery, 2 cups chopped parsnip, 1 cup chopped leek, 12 black peppercorns, 4 unpeeled garlic cloves, 3 bay leaves, 1 basil sprig, 1 thyme sprig, 1 rosemary sprig, 1 parsley sprig, and 5 quarts cold water in an 8-quart stockpot. Bring to a boil; reduce heat, and simmer, uncovered, 3 hours. Strain mixture through a cheesecloth-lined colander into a large bowl, pressing vegetables with the back of a spoon to remove as much liquid as possible; discard solids. Stir in 1 teaspoon table salt. Makes 12 cups. You can store the broth in refrigerator in an airtight container for up to one week, or pour 2 cups broth into freezer-safe containers; freeze for up to three months.

VEGETABLE SOUP
WITH BASIL PESTO,
PAGE 36

CARROT-APPLE
SOUP, PAGE 33

ROASTED CARROTS WITH TOMATO COULIS, PAGE 37

VEGETABLE SOUP WITH BASIL PESTO

A lively vegetable-filled soup is the ultimate celebration of winter's departure. The basil pesto brightens up each spoonful. Instead of using purchased vegetable broth, try making your own (see recipe on page 33).

MAKES 10 CUPS   HANDS-ON 45 MINUTES   TOTAL 60 MINUTES, INCLUDING PESTO

2 medium carrots, chopped

2 celery ribs, chopped

1 large sweet onion, chopped

4 garlic cloves, minced

1 tsp. minced fresh thyme

1 Tbsp. olive oil

2 (32-oz.) containers organic vegetable broth

2 plum tomatoes, seeded and chopped

1 medium zucchini, chopped

1¼ tsp. kosher salt

½ tsp. freshly ground black pepper

1 (15-oz.) can cannellini beans, drained and rinsed

½ cup uncooked mini farfalle (bow-tie) pasta

Basil Pesto

1. Sauté carrots and next 4 ingredients in hot oil in a Dutch oven over medium-high heat 8 to 10 minutes or until vegetables are tender. Stir in broth, tomatoes, zucchini, salt, and black pepper; bring to a boil. Reduce heat to medium-low, and simmer, stirring occasionally, 10 minutes.

2. Stir in beans and pasta, and cook, stirring occasionally, 10 to 12 minutes or until pasta is tender. Top each serving with 1 to 2 teaspoons Basil Pesto.

BASIL PESTO

MAKES ABOUT ½ CUP   HANDS-ON 15 MINUTES   TOTAL 15 MINUTES

2 cups firmly packed fresh basil leaves

½ cup grated Parmesan cheese

3 Tbsp. extra virgin olive oil

1 garlic clove, chopped

½ tsp. kosher salt

Process all ingredients in a food processor until finely ground. Refrigerate in an airtight container up to 1 week.

ROASTED CARROTS WITH TOMATO COULIS

If only carrots and tomatoes were in season at the same time. The sweetness of roasted carrots with the zippy tang of tomatoes works so well together. To get around the calendar that seems to be working against this wonderful flavor combination, I've taken advantage of boxed all-natural tomatoes. Look for them near the canned tomatoes.

MAKES 6 SERVINGS   HANDS-ON 30 MINUTES   TOTAL 1 HOUR

4 lb. carrots with tops

⅓ cup extra virgin olive oil, divided

1 tsp. table salt, divided

½ tsp. freshly ground black pepper, divided

2 garlic cloves, minced

1 yellow onion, finely chopped

1 (26.46-oz.) box chopped tomatoes

⅓ cup red wine vinegar

⅛ tsp. ground red pepper

1 Tbsp. light brown sugar

Garnish: fresh basil

1. Preheat oven to 400°F. Cut tops off carrots, leaving a green sprig of about 1 inch attached to the carrot. Arrange in a single layer on 2 jelly-roll pans. Toss carrots with ¼ cup olive oil. Sprinkle with ½ teaspoon salt and ¼ teaspoon black pepper. Roast at 400°F for 45 minutes, turning once, or until golden brown.

2. Heat remaining olive oil in a large skillet over medium-low heat. Add garlic and onion; cook 10 minutes or until translucent. Add tomatoes, remaining ½ teaspoon salt and ¼ teaspoon black pepper, and next 3 ingredients. Cook for 25 minutes or until thickened. Keep warm. Serve tomato coulis spooned over carrots.

NOTE: I tested with Pomi Chopped Tomatoes.

sage advice

When buying vegetables with the tops, look for fresh, lively, colorful leaves and stems. Separate the tops and the roots for storage. The tops will deprive the vegetable of flavor and nutrients. Save the tops and add them to salads, sautés, or soups.

—Michelle Weaver,
executive chef of Charleston Grill, Charleston, SC

LAYERED CARROT CAKE

Pineapple and freshly grated carrot sing of spring sweetness. Nothing is sacrificed in this lightened-up cream cheese frosting; it's just as decadent as you always remembered.

MAKES 16 SERVINGS   HANDS-ON 30 MINUTES   TOTAL 2 HOURS

BATTER

3 cups all-purpose flour

1 cup plus 2 Tbsp. granulated sugar

3 tsp. baking soda

1½ tsp. ground cinnamon

1½ tsp. table salt

1½ (8-oz.) cans crushed pineapple in juice, drained

⅓ cup vegetable oil

3 large eggs

3 large egg whites

1½ Tbsp. vanilla extract

4½ cups grated carrots

Vegetable cooking spray

FROSTING

1 (8-oz.) package ⅓-less-fat cream cheese

¼ cup butter, softened

2 tsp. vanilla extract

6 cups powdered sugar

2 to 4 tsp. fat-free milk (optional)

1. Prepare Batter: Preheat oven to 350°F. Combine first 5 ingredients in a large bowl; make a well in center of mixture. Whisk together pineapple and next 4 ingredients; add pineapple mixture to flour mixture, stirring just until dry ingredients are moistened. Fold in carrots. Pour batter into 2 greased (with cooking spray) and floured (8-inch) round cake pans.

2. Bake at 350°F for 22 to 25 minutes or until a wooden pick inserted in center comes out clean. Cool in pans on a wire rack 10 minutes. Remove from pans to a wire rack; cool completely (about 1 hour).

3. Prepare Frosting: Beat first 3 ingredients at medium speed with an electric mixer until smooth. Gradually add powdered sugar to butter mixture; beat at low speed just until blended. (Do not overbeat.) If desired, beat in up to 4 teaspoons milk to desired consistency. Place 1 cake layer on a serving plate; spread with ⅔ cup frosting, and top with remaining cake layer. Spread remaining frosting over top and sides of cake.

VEGETABLE GARDENING 101

There's nothing quite like picking a vegetable you grew yourself, cooking it just the way you like, and enjoying every bite of it. It's full-cycle satisfaction that yields flavors like no other. Vegetables prefer at least six hours a day of full sun. Leafy vegetables, like lettuce or collards, require slightly less. Make sure the soil has good drainage, or opt for raised beds or containers for less-perfect locations. Water to keep the soil moist, not soggy. Keep weeds at bay and the soil moist by using pine straw or wood mulch (do not use cypress mulch). Use organic fertilizer, and put your compost from the winter to work boosting the soil.

When planting your first garden, opt for vegetables that are easy to grow and produce plenty to savor. Yellow crookneck squash and zucchini take off without much care. Okra grows straight up and will bless the gardener with pods to pick nearly every day. Jalapeños and other small peppers are also good choices for helping thumbs to green-up.

Timing your vegetable planting perfectly means working around the first and last frosts. Most fall and winter crops do best planted about two months before the first frost. Spring crops are planted about six weeks before the last frost. Summer crops like to be planted after the last frost has passed.

English Peas

How an English pea got its name is a bit of a modern-day mystery, especially since it originated in Asia. The little green gem may not have been named until being cooked in the American colonies as a nod back home to England.

Thomas Jefferson, an early pea aficionado, grew more than 25 pea varieties at Monticello. For better or for worse, English peas were the first vegetable to be canned. Although they are most often enjoyed in frozen or canned forms, a fresh-from-the-pod English pea will nearly leave you speechless. The season is short and sweet while the pods ripen from the bottom of the plant up.

Pods should be plump and moist—a pea or a pod that appears dry has passed its prime. Pods should feel heavy and shouldn't have any peas rattling inside. High sugar content converts to starch within hours of picking, so cook them quickly once you get them home, and enjoy every bite.

Store them in the refrigerator in an open bag for up to two days. When shopping the market for a particular recipe, keep in mind that 1 pound of English peas in the pods equals about 1 cup of shelled peas.

CHILLED SWEET PEA SOUP WITH MINT AND CREAM

This soup is perfect for spring parties since it can be made up to two days in advance. The vibrant green color from fresh peas brightens up a menu instantly. Roasted salmon or grilled shrimp would be right at home with this peppy soup.

MAKES 1½ QUARTS   HANDS-ON 30 MINUTES   TOTAL 1 HOUR

2 Tbsp. butter

3 medium leeks (white and light green parts only), rinsed, drained, and chopped

1 (32-oz.) container reduced-sodium fat-free chicken broth

1 lb. fresh sweet peas

¼ cup chopped fresh mint leaves

2 tsp. kosher salt

½ tsp. freshly ground black pepper

1 cup sour cream

2 Tbsp. fresh lemon juice

Garnish: sliced chives

1. Melt butter in a large saucepan over medium-low heat. Add leeks, and cook, stirring occasionally, 6 to 8 minutes or until tender. Stir in chicken broth, and increase heat to high. Bring to a boil. Add peas, and cook, stirring occasionally, 2 to 3 minutes or until peas are tender. Remove from heat, and stir in mint, salt, and pepper.

2. Process pea mixture, in batches, in a blender or food processor until smooth. Transfer mixture to a bowl, and whisk in ½ cup sour cream. Season with salt and pepper, and pour into 2-ounce glasses. Chill 30 minutes to 1 hour. Whisk together lemon juice and remaining ½ cup sour cream, and dollop on each serving.

LEMON SPRING PEAS WITH SEARED SCALLOPS

Scallops are incredibly quick to cook but really need a skillet that's large enough to give each of them plenty of breathing room to sear. To ensure a golden crust on each scallop, wipe the skillet out between batches. The moisture left from the first batch will keep the second one from searing properly. If you can find pea shoots at the farmers' market, this is a perfect time to show them off as garnish.

MAKES 6 SERVINGS   HANDS-ON 30 MINUTES   TOTAL 35 MINUTES

2 cups fresh green peas

2 Tbsp. unsalted butter

1 cup diced Vidalia onion

1 garlic clove, minced

Zest of 1 lemon

1 Tbsp. chopped fresh chives

1 Tbsp. chopped fresh flat-leaf parsley

½ tsp. table salt

¼ tsp. freshly ground black pepper

2 lb. sea scallops

¼ cup olive oil

Garnish: fresh chives

1. Bring a large pot of water to a boil. Blanch peas 2 minutes or until just tender. Plunge peas into ice water to stop the cooking process; drain.

2. Heat 1 tablespoon butter in a large skillet over medium heat. Add onion and garlic, and cook for 4 to 5 minutes or until softened. Reduce heat to medium-low. Add peas, lemon zest, and next 4 ingredients, and stir to incorporate. Cook, covered, for 5 minutes. Stir in remaining 1 tablespoon butter. Keep warm.

3. Pat scallops dry with a paper towel. Heat a large cast-iron skillet over medium-high heat. Once hot, add 2 tablespoons olive oil. Working in batches, carefully add scallops to pan, and cook 3 minutes on each side or until deeply browned. Before cooking second batch, carefully wipe out skillet with paper towels. Repeat with remaining 2 tablespoons olive oil and second batch of scallops. Serve scallops immediately with peas.

SPRING PEA ORZO

Add the dressing to the orzo while it's still warm, which allows the flavor to soak into the pasta. The colorful salad only gets better the next day, so save some time and make it ahead.

MAKES 6 SERVINGS   HANDS-ON 20 MINUTES   TOTAL 1 HOUR, 30 MINUTES

3 to 4 lemons

8 oz. uncooked orzo pasta

¼ cup minced shallot or red onion

2 Tbsp. extra virgin olive oil

1 Tbsp. Dijon mustard

½ tsp. table salt

½ tsp. freshly ground black pepper

1½ cups cooked fresh or frozen peas

1 cup snow peas or sugar snap peas, blanched and chopped

1 cup assorted chopped fresh herbs (I used mint, chives, and parsley)

½ cup sliced almonds, toasted

1. Grate zest from lemons to equal 2 teaspoons; set aside. Cut lemons in half; squeeze juice from lemons to equal ½ cup.

2. Prepare pasta according to package directions. Whisk together shallots, next 4 ingredients, and lemon juice. Toss together pasta and shallot mixture. Cover with plastic wrap, and chill 1 to 48 hours.

3. Toss together pasta, peas, snow peas, herbs, almonds, and lemon zest just before serving. Add salt, pepper, and additional lemon juice to taste.

Fennel

This slow-growing, crisp bulb, a member of the parsley family, is reminiscent of anise, with its licorice-like flavor. It's normally purchased whole, complete with feathery fronds and a very long stem. The bulbs have a crisp texture and are the most commonly used portion of the vegetable. Larger fennel bulbs are usually more tender than smaller, skinnier ones. Sliced bulbs are often added to salads raw but can be roasted and sautéed. Use the entire vegetable by garnishing with fennel flowers, and treat the fronds like you would dill. If chopping in advance, add a little lemon juice to keep the pieces from browning.

Choose fennel that is firm with no wilting. The core on the bottom of the bulb should be tender when pressed. Store the bulbs separate from the fronds in an open bag for up to one week in the refrigerator.

FENNEL-AND-POTATO GRATIN

This rich and beautiful side dish is a lovely addition to an Easter menu of ham or lamb. The cheesy layers satisfy both adults and children.

MAKES 8 SERVINGS   HANDS-ON 30 MINUTES   TOTAL 1 HOUR, 22 MINUTES

3 Tbsp. butter

1 shallot, sliced

1 garlic clove, minced

2 Tbsp. all-purpose flour

1¼ cups half-and-half

½ (10-oz.) block sharp white
   Cheddar cheese, shredded

½ tsp. table salt

¼ tsp. freshly ground black
   pepper

⅛ tsp. ground nutmeg

2 large russet potatoes (about
   2 lb.), peeled and thinly
   sliced

1 small fennel bulb, thinly
   sliced

Garnish: fresh rosemary sprigs

1. Preheat oven to 400°F. Melt butter in a heavy saucepan over medium heat. Add shallot; sauté 2 to 3 minutes or until tender. Add garlic, and sauté 1 minute.

2. Whisk in flour; cook, whisking constantly, 1 minute. Gradually whisk in half-and-half; cook, whisking constantly, 3 to 4 minutes or until thickened and bubbly. Remove from heat. Whisk in cheese until melted and smooth. Stir in salt and next 2 ingredients.

3. Layer potato and fennel slices alternately in a lightly greased, broiler-safe ceramic 2-quart casserole dish. Spread cheese sauce over layers. Cover with aluminum foil.

4. Bake at 400°F for 50 minutes or until potatoes are tender. Remove from oven. Increase oven temperature to broil with oven rack 5 inches from heat. Uncover dish, and broil 2 to 4 minutes or until golden brown.

SKIRT STEAK WITH FENNEL SLAW

Fennel brings a light and bright flavor to a grilled skirt steak. Skirt steak is packed with flavor and is super-tender after marinating. It's a mainstay at our house. Try adding corn tortillas on the grill for impromptu tacos.

MAKES 4 SERVINGS   HANDS-ON 30 MINUTES   TOTAL 1 HOUR

STEAK

⅓ cup red wine vinegar

⅓ cup extra virgin olive oil

4 garlic cloves, minced

½ tsp. Dijon mustard

½ tsp. table salt

½ tsp. freshly ground black pepper

1½ lb. skirt steak

FENNEL SLAW

1¼ cups thinly sliced fennel bulb

¼ cup sliced green onions

2 Tbsp. thinly sliced celery

1 Tbsp. mayonnaise

2 Tbsp. fresh lime juice

1 Tbsp. chopped fresh cilantro

1 tsp. diced jalapeño pepper

1 tsp. red wine vinegar

⅛ tsp. table salt

⅛ tsp. freshly ground black pepper

1. Prepare Steak: Preheat grill to 350° to 400°F (medium-high) heat. In a large zip-top plastic bag, combine the vinegar, olive oil, garlic, mustard, salt, and pepper. Shake to combine. Add steak to the bag, seal bag, and marinate 30 minutes. Remove steak from marinade, discarding marinade.

2. Grill steak, turning once, 10 minutes for medium-rare. Let steak rest for 10 minutes before slicing.

3. Prepare Fennel Slaw: Combine all ingredients. Chill until ready to serve.

4. Slice each strip of steak in half to make 2 shorter strips. Slice down the long side (across the grain) of each strip to create ½-inch-thick slices. Serve with slaw.

sage advice

Many Southern cooks grew up learning to peel celery to remove the tough strings on the outer layer of the stalks. Stringing celery has gotten less common with the step being skipped more and more frequently. If serving celery raw or in larger pieces, I like to use a "Y" peeler to remove the long fibrous strings. When I finely chop it for cooking, I save a little time and omit the peeling.

WILD RICE WITH BACON AND FENNEL

This warm side dish takes the chill off evenings in the early spring. Golden raisins add just enough sweetness to perfectly balance the salty bacon. Serve this with grilled pork tenderloin.

MAKES 8 SERVINGS   HANDS-ON 40 MINUTES   TOTAL 1 HOUR, 5 MINUTES

1⅓ cups uncooked wild rice

4 thick bacon slices

1 large fennel bulb, thinly sliced

1 large onion, cut into thin wedges

2 garlic cloves, minced

½ cup reduced-sodium fat-free chicken broth

⅓ cup golden raisins

¼ tsp. table salt

⅛ tsp. freshly ground black pepper

¼ cup chopped fresh fennel fronds or flat-leaf parsley

1 Tbsp. white wine vinegar

½ cup chopped toasted walnuts

1. Cook wild rice according to package directions; drain.

2. Meanwhile, cook bacon in a large nonstick skillet over medium-high heat 7 to 8 minutes or until crisp; drain on paper towels, reserving 1 tablespoon drippings in skillet. Chop bacon.

3. Sauté fennel bulb and onion in hot drippings over medium-high heat 5 minutes or until softened. Add garlic; sauté 1 minute. Add broth and next 3 ingredients; bring to a boil. Reduce heat to medium-low; cover and simmer 8 minutes or until tender. Stir in rice and bacon; cook, stirring often, 3 minutes.

4. Transfer to a large serving bowl. Stir in fennel fronds and vinegar. Stir in walnuts just before serving.

sage advice

Buy nuts in large quantities and freeze for up to one year. It's much more economical than buying the small packages at the grocery store.

Lettuces

Lettuces have the reputation of just being water-filled leaves, but they offer much more than that. The crispy leaves are filled with vitamins, magnesium, and chromium. There are many types of lettuce, and combining them often has a wonderful effect. Wash leaves just before you're going to use them to prevent wilting. Dry the leaves well. (A watered down dressing can be an unintended effect of wet leaves.) Tear the leaves instead of cutting them to prevent browning.

If your lettuce plant in the garden has raced toward the sky and bolted, the stalk can add great crunch to salads. If the stalk is very woody on the outside, you may need to peel it before chopping it.

In the market, look for heads that are not wilted and that lack any browning. The leaves should be attached firmly to the base.

Store lettuce heads in a loose bag in the refrigerator for three to five days. If possible, simply avoid prechopped bagged lettuces. Once lettuce is chopped, its shelf life is shortened dramatically and crispness is compromised.

GRILLED ROMAINE SALAD

The best way to get out of a salad rut is to put your lettuce on the grill. Romaine is hearty enough to hold up to the heat. Wait until just before serving to grill the lettuce. With a simple dressing of buttermilk and chives, it's a brand new salad day!

MAKES 8 SERVINGS   HANDS-ON 10 MINUTES   TOTAL 21 MINUTES

4 romaine lettuce bunches

1 small red onion

2 Tbsp. olive oil

Vegetable cooking spray

Buttermilk-Chive Dressing

½ cup freshly shaved Parmesan cheese

1. Pull off tough outer leaves of romaine bunches, and discard; cut bunches in half lengthwise, keeping leaves intact. Peel onion, and cut in half vertically, keeping core (root end and top) intact. Cut each half into 4 wedges. Brush lettuce and onion evenly with olive oil.

2. Coat cold cooking grate of grill with cooking spray. Preheat grill to 300° to 350°F (medium) heat. Place onion wedges on cooking grate, and grill, covered with grill lid, 3 to 4 minutes on each side or to desired degree of doneness. Remove onion wedges.

3. Place romaine halves, cut sides down, on cooking grate. Grill, without grill lid, 2 to 3 minutes or just until wilted.

4. Divide grilled lettuce, cut sides up, among serving plates. Top each with 1 onion wedge (separate into slices, if desired), and drizzle with Buttermilk-Chive Dressing. Sprinkle evenly with cheese, and add salt and pepper to taste. Serve immediately.

BUTTERMILK-CHIVE DRESSING

MAKES 1¼ CUPS   HANDS-ON 10 MINUTES   TOTAL 10 MINUTES

¾ cup buttermilk

½ cup mayonnaise

2 Tbsp. chopped fresh chives

1 Tbsp. minced green onion

1 garlic clove, minced

½ tsp. table salt

¼ tsp. freshly ground black pepper

Whisk together all ingredients. Cover and chill until ready to use.

NOTE: Dressing may be stored in an airtight container in the refrigerator up to three days.

ALL THINGS SPRING SALAD

For a light lunch or side to a warm evening's dinner on the screened porch, nothing says spring like this combination. Meyer lemon and mint are perfect pairings to salad greens. The sweet citrus flavor and refreshing herb allow the lettuce flavor to shine instead of being overpowered. Serving the salad on a platter really shows off its beauty.

MAKES 4 SERVINGS   HANDS-ON 30 MINUTES   TOTAL 30 MINUTES

¼ cup fresh Meyer lemon juice

3 Tbsp. extra virgin olive oil

¼ tsp. Dijon mustard

½ tsp. table salt

⅛ tsp. freshly ground black pepper

12 cups mixed salad greens

2 cups thinly sliced fennel

½ cup loosely packed mint leaves

3 avocados, sliced

4 hard-cooked large eggs, peeled

1. Whisk together lemon juice and next 4 ingredients.

2. Arrange lettuce on a platter and top with next 3 ingredients. Slice each egg into fourths and arrange on salad. Drizzle with dressing before serving. Serve any extra dressing on the side.

sage advice

When gently squeezing an avocado, it should be just soft enough to yield slightly. The stem should come off easily, and underneath it should be green.

KENTUCKY BIBB SALAD WITH BOURBON VINAIGRETTE

Impressive corn cakes are served with crisp lettuce tossed with a mix of smoky bacon and sweet peaches, making this a hearty and satisfying salad with the very essence of spring in every forkful.

MAKES 6 SERVINGS   HANDS-ON 30 MINUTES   TOTAL 1 HOUR, 20 MINUTES

1½ cups pecan halves and pieces

2 Tbsp. butter, melted

3 Tbsp. light brown sugar

⅛ tsp. ground red pepper

6 thick bacon slices, cooked and crumbled

8 cups torn Bibb lettuce (2 to 3 medium heads)

4 cups trimmed watercress

4 large peaches, peeled and sliced

1 small red onion, halved and thinly sliced

4 oz. Gorgonzola cheese, crumbled

Bourbon Vinaigrette

Country Ham Corn Cakes

1. Preheat oven to 350°F. Toss pecans in butter. Stir together brown sugar and red pepper in a bowl; add pecans, tossing to coat. Spread in a single layer in a lightly greased aluminum foil-lined shallow pan. Bake at 350°F for 10 to 12 minutes or until toasted and fragrant. Remove from oven; toss with bacon. Cool in pan on a wire rack 20 minutes; separate pecans with a fork.

2. Combine Bibb lettuce, next 3 ingredients, and pecan mixture in a bowl. Top with cheese. Serve with vinaigrette and corn cakes.

BOURBON VINAIGRETTE

Whisk together ⅓ cup apple cider vinegar, 1 teaspoon light brown sugar, 3 tablespoons bourbon, 2 teaspoons Dijon mustard, ¾ teaspoon table salt, and ½ teaspoon black pepper in a medium bowl. Add ⅔ cup canola oil in a slow, steady stream, whisking constantly until smooth. Makes 1¼ cups.

COUNTRY HAM CORN CAKES

Stir together 1 (6 -ounce) package buttermilk cornbread mix and ⅔ cup water until smooth. Stir in ¾ cup fresh corn kernels and ⅓ cup finely chopped country ham. For each corn cake, pour about ¼ cup batter onto a hot, lightly greased griddle. Cook over medium heat for 3 to 4 minutes or until tops are covered with bubbles and edges look dry. Turn and cook other side. Makes 8 servings.

BUILDING A BETTER SALAD

Wonderful salads are a balance of color, texture, shape, flavor, and acidity. You can quickly put together an impressive salad by choosing a mix of greens, nuts, fruit, cheese, and onion. Since each of these play a role in the final flavor, it's best to use ingredients that are at their peak.

Using several different salad greens can make for an interesting arrangement in both flavor and appearance. Toss in your favorite chopped fresh herbs to boost the greens.

When choosing a dressing, a good guideline is less is more. The flavors and the amount used should enhance the salad, not cover it up. Here's a classic vinaigrette recipe to match just about any salad: Whisk together ⅓ cup red wine vinegar, ⅔ cup extra virgin olive oil, 1 teaspoon good Dijon mustard, pinch of chopped herbs, table salt, and freshly ground black pepper.

My favorite choice for adding crunchy texture to a salad is toasted pecans or pine nuts. Sunflower seeds and dried cranberries or raisins also add to the variety in texture. Crisp fruit, like apple or pear slices, are always a refreshing choice.

All ingredients in the salad should be thoroughly dried after washing. (A dressing diluted with excess water won't cling to leaves.) I prefer to make salads arranged on platters so all the ingredients can be on display and dressed without tossing so you don't spoil the look of the salad.

Radishes

For centuries, the French have enjoyed butter and salt with their radishes a lot like we love cheese with crackers. The radishes are often scored on the bottom so a dip into butter soaks into each bite. This classic picnic snack is then sprinkled with fleur de sel, or fine sea salt, before enjoying.

Radishes are vibrant in color and can be the ideal start to a meal. They pair well with so many flavors and can enhance dishes from salads to tacos. In general, the larger the radish, the hotter it is likely to be. If heat is not to your taste, cooking will dull the fiery bite.

The firmer the radish skin is, the fresher it is. Radish greens are slightly spicy and are excellent for salads. Store them well wrapped in the refrigerator so they retain their moisture.

PICKLED RADISHES

Spring doesn't have to end in June. Thanks to pickling and canning, the flavor of the finest radishes can last until the first snowflake falls. Serve these little tangy bursts alongside charcuterie or with pimiento cheese.

MAKES 6 (1-PINT) JARS   HANDS-ON 45 MINUTES
TOTAL 1 HOUR, PLUS 1 WEEK STAND TIME

5 lb. radishes, tops removed

8 cups apple cider vinegar

½ cup table salt

6 garlic cloves, sliced

6 serrano peppers

2 Tbsp. dill seeds

2 Tbsp. mustard seeds

1. Trim radishes; cut into wedges. Bring vinegar, 1 cup water, and salt to a boil in a 4-quart saucepan over medium heat.

2. Pack radishes in 6 (1-pint) hot sterilized jars, filling to ½ inch from top. Add 1 sliced garlic clove, 1 serrano pepper, 1 teaspoon dill seeds, and 1 teaspoon mustard seeds to each jar. Pour hot vinegar mixture over mixture in jars, filling to ½ inch from top. Seal and process as directed (see page 139). Let stand at least 7 days before serving.

GEORGIA SHRIMP AND RADISH SALAD

Shopping for radishes at the farmers' market can bring you a choice selection nearly as endless as the colors of Easter eggs. Using two different radish varieties automatically gives this salad a vibrancy of textures, colors, and flavors.

MAKES 4 SERVINGS   HANDS-ON 20 MINUTES   TOTAL 50 MINUTES

2 lb. unpeeled, large raw shrimp

2 Tbsp. extra virgin olive oil

1 tsp. table salt, divided

¾ tsp. freshly ground black pepper, divided

1 (4-oz.) watermelon radish, cut into fourths and thinly sliced

4 oz. d'Avignon radishes, thinly sliced

4 green onions, sliced

½ cup diced fennel bulb

¼ cup fresh orange juice

1 tsp. honey

1 tsp. Dijon mustard

2 Tbsp. mayonnaise

¼ cup chopped fresh mint

Garnish: fresh mint sprigs

1. Peel and devein shrimp, and pat dry. Sauté in a very hot cast-iron skillet over medium-high heat 4 minutes.

2. Combine shrimp, olive oil, ½ teaspoon salt, ½ teaspoon pepper, and next 4 ingredients in a large bowl.

3. Whisk together orange juice, next 4 ingredients, and remaining ½ teaspoon salt and ¼ teaspoon pepper. Pour over shrimp mixture, and toss. Serve chilled.

✦ sage advice ✦

Radishes should be eaten fresh, as the taste is not only impaired by lying a day or two after they are drawn, but tough and heavy, which makes them hard on digestion, and of course renders them unhealthy.

—Mrs. Lettice Bryan in *The Kentucky Housewife* (1839)

SALMON TOSTADAS WITH ZUCCHINI-RADISH SLAW

Warm-weather weeknight dinners don't get easier than this. In just 35 minutes, the tostadas are as beautiful as they are fast. Serve them with lime wedges and avocados.

MAKES 4 TO 6 SERVINGS   **HANDS-ON 30 MINUTES**   **TOTAL 35 MINUTES**

½ cup sour cream

1 tsp. lime zest

1 garlic clove, minced

¼ tsp. ground chipotle chile pepper

1 Tbsp. fresh lime juice

2½ cups shredded savoy cabbage

1 cup grated zucchini

5 radishes, thinly sliced

⅓ cup loosely packed fresh cilantro leaves

1 jalapeño pepper, thinly sliced

2 Tbsp. olive oil

3 Tbsp. fresh lime juice

1 or 2 (4-oz.) hot-smoked salmon fillets or smoked trout

6 tostada shells

1 avocado

1. Stir together sour cream, lime zest, garlic, ground chipotle chile pepper, 1 tablespoon lime juice, and salt and pepper to taste. Toss together cabbage, zucchini, radishes, cilantro, jalapeño pepper, olive oil, lime juice, and salt and pepper to taste. Let stand 15 minutes.

2. Flake salmon into pieces, discarding skin. Spread sour cream mixture over tostada shells, and top with salmon and cabbage mixture. Cut avocado into 6 wedges. Top tostadas with avocado wedges; serve immediately.

Ramps

Ramps are wild leeks that thrive in the Appalachian Mountains. They can be found at some farmers' markets but often are foraged by cooks craving one of the premium harbingers of spring.

They like to grow in moist soil, so expect a lot of dirt on each one. Have patience when cleaning them; it takes awhile but the time is well worth it. Look for perky ramps that are not wilted and have a vibrant, wide green leaf.

Ramps don't last long, so cook them as soon as possible for the best results.

PICKLED RAMPS

If you love pickled onions, you'll adore this tangy take on ramps. Pickling and then storing them in your refrigerator is a great way to extend their very short season for a bit longer. I love them on barbecue sandwiches and with egg salad for lunch.

MAKES 1¼ CUPS   HANDS-ON 10 MINUTES
TOTAL 40 MINUTES, PLUS 1 DAY FOR CHILLING

8 oz. ramps, cleaned of soil, leaves trimmed 1-inch from the top of the pink area

¾ cup white wine vinegar

¼ cup sugar

¼ tsp. table salt

½ tsp. whole tricolored peppercorns

¼ tsp. fennel seeds

¼ tsp. mustard seeds

¼ tsp. celery seeds

1. Bring 1 inch of water to a boil in a large skillet. Add ramps and cook for 45 seconds. Plunge ramps into ice water to stop the cooking process. Once cooled, place in a pint-sized jar.

2. Heat vinegar and remaining ingredients in a saucepan over medium heat, stirring constantly. Cook for 2 minutes or until sugar dissolves. Pour over ramps in the jar. Allow to cool for 30 minutes. Cover and refrigerate for 1 day before serving.

sage advice

Not wanting to waste a bit of this one opportunity (with ramps), I washed the roots and then simmered them to make a ramp broth that I used in a soup.

—Deborah Madison from *Vegetable Literacy* (Ten Speed Press, 2013)

BACON AND RAMP JAM

The possibilities are endless with this addictive combination of Southern favorites. Spread it on crackers with cheese, add a spoonful on top of pimiento cheese, and even try it with your favorite fried egg sandwich.

MAKES 1¼ CUPS   HANDS-ON 20 MINUTES   TOTAL 1 HOUR, 20 MINUTES

1 lb. thick hickory-smoked bacon, finely chopped

1 cup diced yellow onion

2 garlic cloves, minced

8 oz. ramps, cleaned of soil, leaves trimmed 1-inch from the top of the pink area, thinly sliced

⅓ cup firmly packed light brown sugar

¼ cup plus 2 Tbsp. apple cider vinegar

1 tsp. mustard seeds

⅛ tsp. freshly ground black pepper

1 Tbsp. good quality bourbon

1. Cook bacon over medium heat in a Dutch oven (I tested with enameled cast iron) for 15 minutes. (Almost all of the bacon will be browned and crispy.) Use a slotted spoon to push bacon to 1 side of the pot. Tilt pot slightly so drippings are on 1 side, reserving 2 tablespoons in Dutch oven.

2. Reduce heat to medium-low. Add onion and garlic to bacon, and cook 3 minutes, stirring often. Add ramps, and cook for 4 minutes. Reduce heat to low. Add brown sugar, and stir to coat. Add vinegar, mustard seeds, and black pepper. Simmer, uncovered, 20 minutes, stirring occasionally.

3. Add bourbon, and cook 10 minutes. Remove from heat, and allow to cool. Store, covered, in refrigerator for up to 1 week.

NOTE: I tested with Wright's Naturally Hickory Smoked Sliced Bacon and Jefferson's Bourbon.

sage advice

It can be difficult to measure pepper when grinding with a handheld pepper grinder. For fresh ground pepper that agrees with a measuring spoon, start by buying whole peppercorns in large quantities (like at wholesale clubs). They will last indefinitely before being ground. Grind a few tablespoons at a time in a burr coffee grinder, and store in a small jar.

RAMP AND CHÈVRE TART

Tarts don't get much prettier than this. It's a free-form tart—no special tart pan needed. You can arrange the ramps neatly in a row for a more uniform appearance or scatter them over the top.

MAKES 4 SERVINGS   HANDS-ON 20 MINUTES   TOTAL 1 HOUR, 30 MINUTES

½ (17.3-oz.) package frozen puff pastry sheets, thawed

Parchment paper

¼ cup olive oil

6 oz. ramps, cleaned of soil, roots removed

4 oz. goat cheese, softened

1 oz. Parmigiano-Reggiano cheese, grated

1 large egg yolk

1 tsp. chopped fresh thyme

2 Tbsp. chopped fresh flat-leaf parsley

½ tsp. table salt

½ tsp. freshly ground black pepper

1. Preheat oven to 400°F. On a well-floured surface, roll puff pastry sheet into a 12- x 10-inch rectangle. Transfer to a parchment paper-lined baking sheet. Trim uneven edges of pastry. Use a paring knife to score a 1-inch-thick border around the edges of the pastry rectangle (like a picture frame). Be careful not to cut all the way through the pastry. Use a fork to prick all over the center of the pastry. Chill pastry for 30 minutes.

2. Bake pastry at 400°F for 15 minutes. Cool at least 10 minutes.

3. While pastry is cooling, heat olive oil in a large skillet over medium-low heat. Add ramps and sauté for 5 minutes or until just becoming tender. Remove from heat and set aside.

4. Combine goat cheese and remaining ingredients. Spread on the center of the pastry, making sure to keep the border free of cheese. Arrange ramps on top of cheese mixture. (The ramps will be very limber and will need to be arranged carefully.) Bake at 400°F for 18 to 20 minutes or until pastry is golden brown. Cool for 10 minutes before serving.

Vidalia Onions

The official vegetable of Georgia takes pride in its sweetness. They are hand-planted and hand-harvested. The growing region is only in parts of 20 counties in south Georgia around the town of Vidalia. It legally can't be a Vidalia onion if it's not grown in the area.

These special onions have a high moisture content, which gives them a sweeter flavor but a shorter shelf life. Store them in a way that they won't touch each other, away from light, moisture, and heat. If you remember seeing onions in pantyhose legs hanging in the closet, now you know why.

When choosing them at the store, look for firm onions with the papery skins still attached tightly. To store them long-term, maybe in hopes for these sweeties being on the Christmas table, wrap each one in aluminum foil or newspaper, and place in the refrigerator. You'll lose a few to rot, but most will make it well into the winter months.

BABY VIDALIA SKILLET SOUFFLÉ

A puffy and satisfying start to the day comes in a skillet. Be prepared to serve this soufflé straight from the oven so its airiness can be seen. Choose a well-seasoned cast-iron skillet to make spooning out servings easier. For an extra pretty touch, lay squash blossoms on the top of the soufflé before baking.

MAKES 4 SERVINGS   HANDS-ON 20 MINUTES   TOTAL 35 MINUTES

¼ cup unsalted butter

2 baby Vidalia onions, sliced

6 large eggs, separated

1½ tsp. chopped fresh thyme

½ tsp. table salt

½ tsp. freshly ground black pepper

½ cup finely grated Parmigiano-Reggiano cheese

7 squash blossoms (optional)

1. Preheat oven to 400°F. Heat butter in a 10-inch cast-iron skillet over medium-low heat. Add onions and cook until soft, but not browned, about 5 minutes. Remove from heat. Use a slotted spoon to remove onions, reserving any butter in the skillet. Allow onions to cool.

2. Beat egg whites at high speed with an electric mixer until stiff peaks form. Whisk together egg yolks, thyme, salt, and pepper in a large bowl. Stir in onions and cheese. Fold in egg whites.

3. Gently pour mixture into skillet. Arrange squash blossoms on top, if desired. Bake at 400°F for 15 minutes or until puffed and lightly browned. Serve immediately.

CARAMELIZED VIDALIA AND YOGURT BISCUITS

Blending slow-cooked sweet onions with tangy yogurt makes a moist and dressy biscuit. Right at home stuffed with sausage or served with supper, these biscuits fit any meal.

MAKES 16 BISCUITS   HANDS-ON 40 MINUTES   TOTAL 2 HOURS

¼ cup unsalted butter

2 Vidalia onions (about 1¾ lb.), finely chopped

1 cup whole plain yogurt

¾ cup heavy cream

4 cups self-rising soft-wheat flour (such as White Lily)

1 Tbsp. baking powder

¼ tsp. table salt

¾ cup unsalted butter, cut into ½-inch cubes and chilled

Parchment paper

1. Melt ¼ cup butter in a medium skillet over medium-low heat. Add Vidalia onions. Cook for 35 minutes, stirring often, or until deep golden brown. Remove from heat. Cool to room temperature. (You should have 1 cup caramelized onions.)

2. Preheat oven to 425°F. Stir together yogurt, cream, and onions in a medium bowl. Combine flour, baking powder, and salt in a large bowl. Cut ¾ cup butter into flour mixture with a pastry blender until crumbly and resembles small peas. Add yogurt mixture; stir just until dry ingredients are moistened. Turn dough out onto a well-floured surface, and knead 4 times with lightly floured hands. Pat dough to ¾-inch thickness. Cut with a 2¾-inch round cutter. (Be very careful not to twist the cutter.) Place biscuits about 1 inch apart on a parchment paper-lined baking sheet. (You may need to gather the scraps and re-pat the dough to yield 16 biscuits.)

3. Bake at 425°F for 16 to 18 minutes or until lightly browned.

NOTE: Biscuits may be frozen before baking. Freeze in a single layer on a baking sheet. Once frozen, transfer to a zip-top plastic freezer bag. Bake frozen biscuits at 425°F for 18 to 20 minutes.

CRISPY FRIED SWEET ONION RINGS

Onions rings are a rite of passage for anyone who's spent more than five minutes in the South. They are crunchy on the outside and sweet on the inside and just about addictive. Serve them with anything from burgers to barbecue.

MAKES 6 SERVINGS   HANDS-ON 40 MINUTES   TOTAL 2 HOURS, 40 MINUTES

2 large sweet onions, cut into
    ⅜-inch-thick slices

3 cups buttermilk

Vegetable oil

2 cups all-purpose flour

1 cup plain yellow cornmeal

2 tsp. table salt

½ tsp. ground red pepper

1. Separate onion slices into rings, and place in a 9-inch square baking dish. Pour buttermilk over onion rings. Cover and chill 2 to 24 hours.

2. Pour oil to depth of 2 inches into a Dutch oven; heat to 360°F.

3. Stir together flour and next 3 ingredients in a shallow dish. Dredge onion rings in flour mixture, shaking off excess, and place on a baking sheet. Discard buttermilk.

4. Fry onion rings, in batches, 2 minutes or until golden brown, turning once. Drain on paper towels. Serve onion rings immediately, or keep warm in a 200°F oven until ready to serve.

SWEET ONION PUDDING

A fine beef tenderloin would be hard pressed to find a more perfect side dish.
The sweetness from the onions and the salty cheese are divine. It's prettiest right
out of the oven while it's puffed and airy.

MAKES 8 SERVINGS   HANDS-ON 1 HOUR, 15 MINUTES   TOTAL 1 HOUR, 45 MINUTES

½ cup butter

6 medium-size sweet onions
    (3¼ pounds), thinly sliced
    and separated into rings

2 cups whipping cream

1 (3-oz.) package shredded
    Parmesan cheese

6 large eggs, lightly beaten

3 Tbsp. all-purpose flour

2 Tbsp. sugar

2 tsp. baking powder

1 tsp. table salt

Garnish: fresh thyme leaves

1. Melt butter in a large skillet over medium heat; add onion.
Cook, stirring often, about 1 hour or until caramel colored.
Remove from heat.

2. Preheat oven to 350°F. Stir together cream, cheese, and eggs in
a large bowl. Combine flour and next 3 ingredients; gradually stir
into egg mixture.

3. Stir onion into egg mixture; spoon into a lightly greased
13- x 9-inch baking dish. Bake, uncovered, at 350°F for
30 to 32 minutes or until slightly firm, puffed, and golden.

Summer

There is no finer time to cook in the South than during the summer's sizzling dog days. Nearly every color of the rainbow can be found in the bounty of the season.

Corn

We can thank the Mayans for the crop that is now the third largest grown in the world for human consumption. The Native Americans educated pilgrims on how to grow maize, as they called it. Hundreds of years later, Southern cuisine wouldn't be the same without it. Not only do we rely on corn for our all-important staple of grits, we also like to cream it, fry it, eat it raw in salads, and add it to stews. Keep the husks attached to use as handles when eating corn on the cob. Use a clean toothbrush to gently remove silks from the kernels.

Choose corn with silks that are blonde because the silks darken as the corn ages. Most shoppers check the plumpness of the kernels by peeling back the husks a tiny bit to see the kernels, but you can also give the corn a squeeze to see if the kernels are plump. It's best to leave on the husks until you're ready to use the corn to keep it as moist as possible.

Corn should be cooked as soon as possible after picking because the sugars begin converting to starch very quickly. Store fresh corn up to one day in the refrigerator in an open bag.

CREAMED CORN

Real creamed corn should be milky, creamy, and perfectly salty. If the corn isn't the freshest possible, you may need to add a little water at a time as it cooks to keep it from drying out. Use a corn creamer for the creamiest corn or simply cut the kernels from the cob for more texture (as seen in the photo on page 86).

MAKES 6 TO 8 SERVINGS   **HANDS-ON 40 MINUTES**   **TOTAL 40 MINUTES**

13 ears fresh corn, husked
¼ to ½ cup heavy cream
1 Tbsp. unsalted butter
½ tsp. table salt
⅛ tsp. freshly ground black
    pepper
Minced chives (optional)

1. Cut kernels from cobs to yield 6 cups; discard cobs. Cook kernels in a small Dutch oven over low heat, stirring often, about 30 minutes or until corn is tender. (To prevent corn from drying out, add up to 10 tablespoons water, 1 tablespoon at a time as needed, during last 15 minutes of cook time.)

2. Stir in cream and butter, and cook, stirring occasionally, about 5 minutes or until mixture reaches desired consistency. Stir in salt and pepper. Sprinkle with chives, if desired.

⁂ put 'em up ⁂

This light and summery corn broth is a perfect use for corncobs after all the kernels are long gone. Bring 6 corncobs and 8 cups water to a light boil in a Dutch oven over medium-high heat. Reduce heat to low, and simmer 30 minutes. Stir in ½ teaspoon salt. Pour broth through a fine wire-mesh strainer into a large glass bowl, discarding cobs and pulp. Cover and let cool 1 hour or to room temperature. Store in an airtight container in refrigerator up to one week, or freeze up to two months. Makes 6 cups.

CORN-AND-CRAB
CHOWDER, PAGE 89

CREAMED CORN,
PAGE 85

BALSAMIC CORN
SALAD, PAGE 88

BALSAMIC CORN SALAD

When corn is at its peak, there are few things better. With just a simple dressing, a colorful and bright side dish is created. This salad can be made ahead, so it's ideal for warm-weather parties and picnics. The light hue of white balsamic vinegar keeps the colors vibrant.

MAKES 4 TO 6 SERVINGS   HANDS-ON 14 MINUTES   TOTAL 4 HOURS, 44 MINUTES

1 Tbsp. extra virgin olive oil
3½ cups fresh corn kernels
    (about 8 ears)
¼ cup extra virgin olive oil
3 Tbsp. white balsamic vinegar
½ tsp. Dijon mustard
¼ tsp. table salt
⅛ tsp. freshly ground black
    pepper
1 cup diced tomatoes
1 cup packed arugula

1. Heat 1 tablespoon olive oil over medium heat in a large sauté pan. Add corn kernels; cook 4 minutes, stirring often. Cool to room temperature.

2. Whisk together ¼ cup olive oil and next 4 ingredients until combined.

3. Transfer cooled corn to a medium bowl. Add tomatoes. Pour dressing over mixture, and stir well. Chill for 4 hours. Add arugula just before serving.

⤙ sage advice ⤚

Native Americans planted what was known as the Three Sisters Garden of corn, beans, and squash. The vegetables grew perfectly beside each other. The corn provided a natural trellis for the beans to climb on and the large leaves of the squash shaded the soil for coolness.

CORN-AND-CRAB CHOWDER

My family and I love to stop at our favorite roadside stand for fresh Silver Queen corn on the way to the beach. It doesn't take long to simmer the sweet kernels with fresh-from-the-Atlantic crabs for a summer soup tradition.

MAKES 10 CUPS   HANDS-ON 20 MINUTES   TOTAL 1 HOUR, 15 MINUTES

6 bacon slices

2 celery ribs, diced

1 medium-size green bell
   pepper, diced

1 medium onion, diced

1 jalapeño pepper, seeded
   and diced

1 (32-oz.) container chicken
   broth

3 Tbsp. all-purpose flour

3 cups fresh corn kernels
   (about 6 ears)

1 lb. fresh lump crabmeat,
   drained and picked free
   of shell*

1 cup whipping cream

¼ cup chopped fresh cilantro

½ tsp. table salt

¼ tsp. freshly ground black
   pepper

Oyster crackers

Garnish: chopped fresh
   cilantro

1. Cook bacon in a Dutch oven over medium heat 8 to 10 minutes or until crisp; remove bacon, and drain on paper towels, reserving 2 tablespoons drippings in Dutch oven. Crumble bacon.

2. Sauté celery and next 3 ingredients in hot drippings 5 to 6 minutes or until tender. Whisk together broth and flour until smooth. Add to celery mixture. Stir in corn. Bring to a boil; reduce heat, and simmer, stirring occasionally, 30 minutes. Gently stir in crabmeat and next 4 ingredients; cook 4 to 5 minutes or until thoroughly heated. Serve warm with crumbled bacon and oyster crackers.

*1 pound peeled cooked shrimp or chopped cooked chicken may be substituted.

OKRA-AND-CORN MAQUE CHOUX

Maque choux is a stewed corn dish that is believed to have originated with Native Americans and made famous by Cajuns. Choose sausage that fits your degree of spiciness. The summer's finest fresh produce gives this Louisiana classic loads of color.

MAKES 8 SERVINGS   HANDS-ON 28 MINUTES   TOTAL 28 MINUTES

¼ lb. spicy smoked sausage, diced

½ cup chopped sweet onion

½ cup chopped green bell pepper

2 garlic cloves, minced

3 cups fresh corn kernels

1 cup sliced fresh okra

1 cup peeled, seeded, and diced tomato (½ lb.)

1. Sauté sausage in a large skillet over medium-high heat 3 minutes or until browned.

2. Add onion, bell pepper, and garlic, and sauté 5 minutes or until tender. Add corn, okra, and tomato; cook, stirring often, 10 minutes. Add salt and pepper to taste.

NOTE: I tested with Conecuh Original Spicy and Hot Smoked Sausage.

FREEZER FACTS

It's often in the peak of the season that the harvest is too plentiful to enjoy right away. An easy way to save some of the crop for later is to freeze any extra you have.

A good general rule to follow is that the smaller the vegetable, the better it freezes. When you're working with larger vegetables, like butternut squash, simply cut them into pieces no larger than ½ inch. Blanching vegetables before freezing helps retain their color and prevents the dreaded freezer browning. It also helps hold in more of the fresh flavor than simply freezing alone. To blanch, simply drop the vegetables into boiling water for 1 to 2 minutes, then plunge them into ice water to stop the cooking process. Once the vegetables have cooled to room temperature, spread them in a single layer on a baking sheet and freeze. Transfer the frozen pieces to a zip-top freezer bag, press out any air, and freeze for up to three months. Label the bag with the date, the vegetable, and the weight.

With field peas often overflowing in the summer, it's usually necessary to freeze several batches. The process is very similar to freezing other vegetables. Cook the shelled peas in boiling water for 2 minutes, drain, and plunge into ice water. Drain and transfer into a zip-top freezer bag, press out any air, and freeze for up to six months.

Cucumbers

Cucumbers originated in India and possess a bit of a cooling sensation. Most people think of two types of cucumbers: pickling and slicing. The difference is easily seen. Slicing cucumbers have mostly smooth skins while pickling ones are usually more bumpy. Both skins are edible but if you eat the skin, make sure that you buy unwaxed cucumbers. The seeds in cucumbers are edible, but they're known to have some noisy side effects on digestive tracks. If you'd rather go seedless, simply scoop them out with a small spoon, or use an English cucumber, which is nearly seedless.

Look for smaller cucumbers that are firm and unwrinkled. Older, larger cucumbers can be bitter. Many historic recipes call for sprinkling the sliced cucumbers with salt to draw out the bitterness,which is a good idea if you're using a larger cucumber.

Store cucumbers loosely wrapped in the produce drawer in the refrigerator for up to three days.

CREAMY CUCUMBER SOUP

I love a chilled soup in the summertime. Cucumbers and Greek yogurt create
a refreshing make-ahead, no-cook option for luncheons and brunches.
Serve it aside a scoop of chicken salad.

MAKES 2 QUARTS   HANDS-ON 20 MINUTES   TOTAL 4 HOURS, 20 MINUTES

¾ cup chicken broth

3 green onions

2 Tbsp. white vinegar

½ tsp. table salt

¼ tsp. freshly ground black
    pepper

3 large English cucumbers
    (about 2½ lb.), peeled,
    seeded, chopped, and
    divided

3 cups fat-free Greek yogurt*

Garnishes: toasted slivered
    almonds, freshly ground
    black pepper, chopped red
    bell pepper

1. Process chicken broth, green onions, vinegar, salt, pepper,
and half of chopped cucumbers in a food processor until smooth,
stopping to scrape down sides.

2. Add yogurt, and pulse until blended. Pour into a large bowl; stir
in remaining chopped cucumbers. Cover and chill 4 to 24 hours.
Add salt to taste just before serving.

*Plain low-fat yogurt may be substituted. Decrease chicken broth
to ½ cup.

CUCUMBER-AND-TOMATO SALAD

A tangy dressing highlights the best of fresh summer produce in this colorful make-ahead salad. Versions of it have been enjoyed at church potlucks and family reunions for years. With no peeling or cooking needed, it's as laid-back as the season.

MAKES 2 CUPS   HANDS-ON 10 MINUTES   TOTAL 3 HOURS, 10 MINUTES

2 cucumbers
3 small tomatoes
1 small green bell pepper
1 small red onion
⅓ cup vegetable oil
3 Tbsp. sugar
3 Tbsp. red wine vinegar
¾ tsp. table salt
⅛ tsp. freshly ground black
   pepper
Garnish: fresh basil

1. Cut cucumbers and tomatoes in half. Remove seeds. Chop cucumber, tomato, bell pepper, and onion.

2. Whisk together oil and next 4 ingredients in a large bowl until sugar dissolves. Add cucumber mixture, tossing to coat. Cover and chill 3 hours.

SPICY ICEBOX PICKLES

Icebox refers to pickles that stay in the refrigerator, instead of those that are canned and ready for months of storage in your pantry. These pickles are fresh and crisp, all while being very easy to make. For the thinnest slices of cucumbers, try using a mandoline.

MAKES 4 CUPS   HANDS-ON 20 MINUTES   TOTAL 20 MINUTES, PLUS 1 DAY FOR CHILLING

2 cups white vinegar
1 cup sugar
2 dried bay leaves
1 tsp. table salt
2 tsp. whole black peppercorns
¾ lb. cucumber
½ medium white onion
2 red chile peppers
1 jalapeño pepper
2 serrano peppers

1. Bring vinegar and next 4 ingredients to a boil in a medium saucepan. Stir to dissolve sugar. Remove from heat.

2. Cut cucumber into ⅛-inch-thick slices (about 3½ cups slices). Thinly slice onion into quarter rounds (1 cup slices). Thinly slice peppers, leaving seeds intact.

3. Divide vegetables between 2 (16-ounce) jars. Carefully pour vinegar mixture over vegetables to fill jars. Screw the lids on jars and chill 1 day before serving. Store pickles in refrigerator up to 1 week.

Eggplant

When eggplants were first grown in China, they were believed to be poisonous. Since then, not only has the vegetable been proven to be nontoxic, but it's also grown into a versatile and unique Southern favorite. There are several varieties, each one as beautiful as the next. Similar to cucumbers, the older the eggplant, the more likely it will be bitter. Bitterness in eggplant can also come from being stored too long in the refrigerator. If bitterness is a problem, sprinkle salt on the slices to neutralize the taste.

When shopping, choose an eggplant that feels heavy for its size and is free of soft spots. Place eggplants in a paper bag before refrigerating to give them a little insulation from the cold in the refrigerator. Use them within four days.

GRILLED, FOLDED, AND FILLED EGGPLANT

My family can't seem to get enough eggplant each summer. I haven't found a way we don't like it cooked. This is a dressy way to serve it as a luncheon entrée or knife-and-fork appetizer for a gathering around the grill. Choose an eggplant that is round and wide for slices large enough to fold.

MAKES 4 MAIN-DISH SERVINGS OR 8 SIDE-DISH SERVINGS
HANDS-ON 10 MINUTES   TOTAL 40 MINUTES

1 (1¾-lb.) eggplant

1 cup extra virgin olive oil

⅓ cup red wine vinegar

1 tsp. Dijon mustard

1 tsp. table salt

1 tsp. freshly ground black
   pepper

2 garlic cloves, minced

2 Tbsp. chopped fresh oregano

1 Tbsp. capers

8 oz. fresh mozzarella cheese,
   sliced into 8 slices

1. Preheat grill to 350° to 400°F (medium-high) heat. Cutting lengthwise, slice eggplant into 8 (½-inch-thick) slices, discarding the two ends.

2. Whisk together olive oil and next 7 ingredients; set aside.

3. Grill eggplant, without grill lid, for 6 to 8 minutes, turning once, or until grill marks form. Pour olive oil mixture into a jelly-roll pan. Remove eggplant directly from the grill and place in marinade, turning to coat. Marinate 10 minutes, turning often.

4. Remove eggplant from marinade, reserving ¼ cup marinade. Fold 1 slice of eggplant over 1 slice of cheese, and arrange on a piece of heavy-duty aluminum foil. Grill, covered with grill lid, for 10 minutes or until cheese is melted. Drizzle with reserved marinade before serving.

EGGPLANT AND ROASTED PEPPER FRITTATA

I love to make this frittata for a weeknight supper when there's little time to spare. Make sure your skillet is ovenproof for a trip under the broiler.

MAKES 6 SERVINGS   HANDS-ON 8 MINUTES   TOTAL 25 MINUTES

2 cups peeled and chopped
   eggplant
3 Tbsp. olive oil
1 (12-oz.) jar or 2 (7-oz.) jars
   roasted red bell peppers,
   drained and chopped
10 large eggs
½ cup milk
1 tsp. table salt
¼ tsp. freshly ground black
   pepper
¼ cup freshly grated Parmesan
   cheese

1. Cook eggplant in olive oil in a 10-inch ovenproof nonstick skillet over medium-high heat, stirring constantly, 2 to 3 minutes or until tender. Stir in roasted red bell peppers.

2. Beat eggs and next 3 ingredients at medium speed with an electric mixer until blended. Add egg mixture to skillet. As mixture starts to cook, gently lift edges of frittata with a spatula, and tilt pan so uncooked portion flows underneath. Cover and cook over low heat 10 to 12 minutes to allow uncooked portion on top to set.

3. Prehat broiler. Uncover, sprinkle with cheese, and broil 3 inches from heat 2 minutes or until golden. Cut into wedges. Serve immediately.

FRIED EGGPLANT

When I was a kid, coming in from playing in the backyard to find a paper towel-lined plate filled with fried eggplant was a really good sign that supper was almost ready. Cornmeal makes each slice crunchy, and I like an extra sprinkle of salt on each one.

MAKES 6 TO 8 SERVINGS   HANDS-ON 33 MINUTES   TOTAL 1 HOUR, 33 MINUTES

2 eggplants, peeled and cut
    into ¼-inch-thick slices
1½ tsp. table salt, divided
1 cup buttermilk
¾ cup self-rising flour
½ cup self-rising cornmeal mix
½ tsp. freshly ground black
    pepper
Vegetable oil
Garnishes: fresh flat-leaf
    parsley, tarragon, sea salt

1. Sprinkle both sides of eggplant slices evenly with 1 teaspoon salt; place on layers of paper towels, and let stand 30 minutes. Rinse and pat dry.

2. Soak eggplant slices in buttermilk about 30 minutes.

3. Combine flour, cornmeal mix, remaining ½ teaspoon salt, and pepper. Drain eggplant slices, and dredge in flour mixture, shaking off excess. Pour oil to depth of 1½ inches in a large cast-iron skillet, and heat to 375°F. Fry eggplant slices 3 minutes or until golden. Drain on paper towels. Serve immediately.

Field Peas & Beans

To say Southerners are proud of their field peas would be an understatement. Often named for their colors, their arrangements in the pod, or the way they cook, field peas can have gloriously eccentric labels. Crowders, lady peas, lady zippers, creamers, pink-eyed purple hulls, butter beans (baby lima beans), and butter peas are just a few of the names. It's practically a rite of passage to shell peas on a front porch during the summer before blanching them to put up for winter.

Choose pods that are firm and unopened. The pods of field peas are inedible. Once shelled, peas can be kept up to three days in the refrigerator, or they can be blanched and frozen for up to six months.

LADY PEA SUMMER SALAD

Having a friend who knows where to get the best field peas is a blessing. Brooke Stortz is a friend of mine who also grew up in a small town and had a grandmother who taught her the value of cooking. She lets me know when lady peas are arriving in town and helps me stay stocked up for winter. I always freeze several quarts for cold-weather cravings.

MAKES 6 SERVINGS   HANDS-ON 11 MINUTES   TOTAL 1 HOUR, 26 MINUTES

1 tsp. table salt
5 cups shelled fresh lady peas
1 medium tomato, chopped
1 small Vidalia onion, diced
3 Tbsp. chopped fresh basil
3 Tbsp. extra virgin olive oil
1 Tbsp. white wine vinegar
1 Tbsp. fresh lemon juice
2 tsp. Dijon mustard

1. Bring 7 cups water to a boil in a large saucepan. Add 1 teaspoon salt. Add peas, and bring back to a boil. Reduce heat to medium, and simmer for about 30 minutes or until tender. Drain and cool to room temperature. Transfer peas to a large bowl. Stir in tomato, onion, and basil.

2. Whisk together olive oil and next 3 ingredients. Add salt and pepper to taste. Pour over peas and stir well. Allow salad to sit for 15 minutes before serving.

NOTE: This salad can be made one day in advance, but add the basil just before serving.

CLASSIC FRESH FIELD PEAS

Each time I serve this home-style recipe, I expect the clock to turn back in time. Ham hocks have been used to flavor Southern vegetables for generations. This is a simple and elegant dish that is reminiscent of the way field peas were meant to be cooked.

MAKES 4 CUPS   HANDS-ON 45 MINUTES   TOTAL 3 HOURS, 10 MINUTES

2 purchased smoked ham hocks

1½ cups finely chopped onion

3 Tbsp. bacon drippings

2 garlic cloves, minced

3 cups shelled fresh field peas (about 1 lb.)

1 tsp. kosher salt

1 tsp. freshly ground black pepper

1. Bring hocks and 2 quarts water to a boil in a large Dutch oven over medium heat; simmer 1½ to 2 hours or until meat is tender.

2. Meanwhile, sauté onion in hot bacon drippings in a medium skillet over medium-high heat 6 minutes. Add garlic; sauté 1 minute.

3. Add peas and onion mixture to Dutch oven with ham hocks; bring to a simmer over medium heat. Cover and simmer, stirring occasionally, 45 minutes or until peas are tender. Remove hocks; drain peas, and sprinkle with salt and pepper.

4. Remove and chop ham from hock bones; discard bones. Stir ham into peas, if desired.

GRILL-SMOKED SUMMER PEAS

The standard baked beans have made a comeback, and they're all dressed up. Smoking fresh field peas on the grill and adding tomatoes and bacon make a version not to be forgotten.

MAKES 6 SERVINGS   HANDS-ON 45 MINUTES   TOTAL 2 HOURS, 25 MINUTES

1 cup hickory wood chips

Vegetable cooking spray

1 lb. fresh shelled field peas or butter beans (about 4 cups)

4 fresh thyme sprigs

1 garlic bulb, cut in half crosswise

1 bay leaf

4 cups boiling water

4 firm, medium-size beefsteak tomatoes, cored

6 bacon slices, chopped

6 garlic cloves, chopped

3 Tbsp. molasses

2 Tbsp. Dijon mustard

2 Tbsp. apple cider vinegar

2 tsp. kosher salt

1 tsp. freshly ground black pepper

1. Soak wood chips in water 30 minutes; drain. Coat cold grill grate with cooking spray. Light 1 side of grill, heating to 400° to 500°F (high) heat; leave other side unlit. Place wood chips in center of a 12-inch square piece of heavy-duty aluminum foil; wrap to form a packet. Pierce several holes in packet; place directly over heat.

2. Combine peas, thyme, garlic, and bay leaf in a 13- x 9-inch disposable aluminum foil pan. Place peas over unlit side of grill and carefully add boiling water. Grill, covered with grill lid, 1 hour or until tender, stirring occasionally. Drain peas, reserving ¾ cup cooking liquid. Discard thyme, garlic bulb, and bay leaf.

3. Halve tomatoes, and grill, covered with grill lid, 2 minutes on each side. Cool 10 minutes. Discard skins; chop tomatoes.

4. Cook bacon in a large saucepan over medium heat, stirring often, 4 minutes or until crisp. Reserve 2 tablespoons drippings in saucepan. Add chopped garlic; sauté 30 seconds. Stir in tomatoes, molasses, and next 2 ingredients; bring to a simmer. Reduce heat to low, and simmer, stirring often, 5 minutes. Stir peas, salt, pepper, and ¾ cup reserved cooking liquid into tomato mixture; cook, stirring often, 10 minutes or until slightly thickened. Adjust seasoning with more vinegar, molasses, salt, and pepper, if desired.

SPECKLED BUTTER BEANS WITH BACON AND BASIL

Speckled butter beans with varying hues of purple and maroon are never to be overlooked. Thanks to their mottled color and mild chestnut flavor, they are sometimes called Christmas Beans. They have been a Southern standard by which many butter beans are judged. The spots and waves of color vanish with heat, and a dark, rich brown butter bean emerges.

MAKES 6 SERVINGS   HANDS-ON 20 MINUTES   TOTAL 1 HOUR, 5 MINUTES

1¼ lb. fresh speckled butter beans
1 tsp. table salt, divided
8 thick bacon slices, chopped
1 red onion, chopped
2 garlic cloves, minced
1 Tbsp. sorghum syrup
¼ cup fresh lemon juice
1 Tbsp. thinly sliced fresh basil

1. Cover beans with water in a medium saucepan over medium heat. Add ½ teaspoon salt, and simmer for 45 to 60 minutes or until tender. Drain.

2. Fry bacon in a large skillet over medium heat until crisp, about 10 minutes. Remove with a slotted spoon and set aside, reserving drippings in pan. Add onion and garlic to drippings; cook for 5 minutes or until translucent. Remove from heat, and stir in sorghum, lemon juice, and remaining ½ teaspoon salt, stirring to loosen browned bits from bottom of pan.

3. Combine butter beans and onion mixture in a large serving bowl. Toss. Top with bacon and basil.

Green Beans

Many Southerners remember green beans referred to as string beans, which means they probably also remember stringing them one by one on a porch on hot afternoons. Green beans can be cooked whole or snapped. Acid tends to turn the bright green color gray, so add any acidic flavors right before serving.

Pole beans are a variety that must be supported on a pole while they're growing. Growing up thin as a rail, I was compared to the famous long and skinny bean on numerous occasions.

Green beans should be crisp and smooth and should snap when broken into pieces. Store them for up to five days in the refrigerator in an open paper bag.

GARDEN GREEN BEAN CASSEROLE

Fresh green beans make the old standard casserole new and exciting. With fresh mushrooms and toasted bread cubes, there's no need for a can opener here!

MAKES 6 TO 8 SERVINGS   **HANDS-ON 30 MINUTES**   **TOTAL 1 HOUR, 15 MINUTES**

2 lb. fresh green beans, trimmed and snapped into 1½-inch pieces

2 cups (½-inch) French bread cubes

2 Tbsp. unsalted butter, melted

4½ Tbsp. unsalted butter, divided

1 (8-oz.) package fresh mushrooms, stemmed and quartered

1 medium onion, thinly sliced

1 garlic clove, minced

1 Tbsp. Worcestershire sauce

3 Tbsp. all-purpose flour

1½ cups milk

1 tsp. table salt

½ tsp. freshly ground black pepper

1. Preheat oven to 375°F. Cook beans in boiling water to cover 10 minutes or until fork-tender; drain. Rinse with cold running water; drain. Transfer to a large bowl.

2. Toss bread with melted butter. Arrange in a jelly-roll pan. Bake at 375°F for 20 minutes or until crisp.

3. Melt 1½ tablespoons butter in a large skillet over medium heat. Add mushrooms, and sauté 4 minutes or until mushrooms have browned and liquid has evaporated. Add onion and garlic, and sauté 3 minutes or until tender. Transfer mixture to bowl with beans. Add Worcestershire sauce to warm skillet, stirring to loosen browned bits from bottom of skillet. Pour sauce over bean mixture.

4. Melt remaining 3 tablespoons butter over medium-low heat in skillet. Add flour, and cook, stirring constantly, 2 minutes. Slowly add milk; cook, stirring constantly, 3 minutes or until thickened. Stir in salt and pepper.

5. Pour white sauce over bean mixture. Stir until well blended, and transfer to a lightly greased 11- x 7-inch baking dish. Top with toasted bread cubes. Bake at 375°F for 15 minutes or until lightly browned.

LEMONY GREEN BEAN PASTA SALAD

Arugula and pistachios are right at home with this cheerful pasta plate. Lemon and shallots marry for a bright taste ideal for a luncheon or light supper.

MAKES 4 TO 6 SERVINGS   HANDS-ON 15 MINUTES   TOTAL 30 MINUTES

12 oz. uncooked casarecce
    pasta*
½ lb. haricots verts (French
    green beans), cut in half
    lengthwise
1 Tbsp. fresh thyme
5 tsp. lemon zest, divided
¼ cup finely chopped roasted
    salted pistachios
2 Tbsp. Champagne vinegar
1 Tbsp. minced shallots
1 garlic clove, minced
1 tsp. table salt
½ tsp. freshly ground black
    pepper
5 Tbsp. olive oil
1½ cups loosely packed arugula
Toppings: roasted salted
    pistachios, Parmesan cheese

1. Cook pasta according to package directions, adding green beans to boiling water during last 2 minutes of cooking time; drain. Rinse pasta mixture with cold running water; drain well.

2. Place pasta mixture, thyme, and 3 teaspoons lemon zest in a large bowl; toss gently to combine.

3. Whisk together ¼ cup pistachios, next 5 ingredients, and remaining 2 teaspoons lemon zest in a small bowl. Add oil in a slow, steady stream, whisking constantly until blended. Drizzle over pasta mixture. Add arugula, and toss gently to coat. Serve with desired toppings.

*Penne pasta may be substituted.

ROASTED GREEN BEAN, APPLE, AND BACON SANDWICHES

Break out of the same sandwich routine with this impressive salad combination that's right at home between slices of baguette. Hollowing out the cut sides of the bread helps to keep the sandwich neat and tidy.

MAKES 8 SERVINGS   HANDS-ON 33 MINUTES   TOTAL 2 HOURS, 33 MINUTES

1 lb. fresh green beans, trimmed

2 tsp. olive oil

¼ tsp. freshly ground black pepper

1 tsp. kosher salt, divided

6 thick bacon slices

½ cup torn fresh dill

½ cup olive oil

1 tsp. firmly packed lemon zest

2 tsp. Dijon mustard

1 small shallot, minced

4 Tbsp. fresh lemon juice, divided

1 medium-size Red Delicious apple

2 (8½-oz.) French bread baguettes, cut in half horizontally

4 oz. Parmigiano-Reggiano cheese, thinly sliced

Wax paper

1. Preheat oven to 425°F. Toss green beans with 2 teaspoons olive oil, pepper, and ¼ teaspoon salt. Place beans in a single layer in a jelly-roll pan, and bake at 425°F for 10 minutes. Remove from oven, transfer to a bowl, and chill 10 minutes.

2. Arrange bacon in a single layer in a jelly-roll pan. Bake at 425°F for 12 minutes or until crisp. Drain on paper towels.

3. Whisk together dill, next 4 ingredients, 3 tablespoons lemon juice, and remaining ¾ teaspoon salt. Let stand 5 minutes.

4. Meanwhile, cut apple into thin slices, and toss with remaining 1 tablespoon lemon juice.

5. Spoon vinaigrette onto top halves of baguettes. Layer beans, bacon, apple, and cheese on bottom halves. Cover with top halves of baguettes; wrap tightly in wax paper. Chill up to 2 hours. Slice sandwiches before serving.

Irish Potatoes

White potatoes, now known as Irish potatoes, originated in South America and flourished as a crop in Europe beginning in the 1600s. By the 1800s much of the Irish population's primary diet consisted of potatoes. When the catastrophic Irish Potato Famine struck in 1845, many Irish immigrants came to America and brought their beloved potato culture with them.

Contrary to belief, potatoes don't like to be stored near onions and garlic. If they keep each other's company too much, they all tend to ripen faster. They prefer a cool, dry, dark place. Organic potatoes will sprout faster than their mainstream counterparts, as many nonorganic potatoes have been treated with sprout inhibitors. If sprouts do occur, pop off or cut out the sprouts and cook the potato as you would normally. Do not eat the sprouts. Cut off any green spots on the potatoes before cooking. Don't waste the skins. With lots of salt, they are divine.

Potatoes should be firm, unwrinkled, and not even slightly spongy.

Compost any leaves you may have if picked from home or the farmers' market.

CARAMELIZED ONION-MASHED POTATO BAKE

Baking mashed potatoes makes serving them to a crowd much easier because they don't have to be served immediately after mashing. The caramelized onions and cheese make this recipe a perfect side dish for neighborhood gatherings.

MAKES 6 TO 8 SERVINGS   HANDS-ON 25 MINUTES   TOTAL 1 HOUR

4 lb. russet potatoes

3 tsp. table salt, divided

1¼ cups warm buttermilk

½ cup warm milk

¼ cup melted butter

½ tsp. freshly ground black pepper

1¼ cups freshly grated Gruyère cheese

1 cup chopped caramelized onions

2 Tbsp. chopped fresh parsley

1. Preheat oven to 350°F. Peel potatoes; cut into 2-inch pieces. Bring potatoes, 2 teaspoons salt, and water to cover to a boil in a large Dutch oven over medium-high heat; boil 20 minutes or until tender. Drain. Return potatoes to Dutch oven, reduce heat to low, and cook, stirring occasionally, 3 to 5 minutes or until potatoes are dry.

2. Mash potatoes with a potato masher to desired consistency. Stir in warm buttermilk, warm milk, melted butter, pepper, and remaining 1 teaspoon salt, stirring just until blended.

3. Stir in Gruyère cheese, caramelized onions, and parsley, and spoon mixture into a lightly greased 2½-quart baking dish or 8 (10-ounce) ramekins. Bake at 350°F for 35 minutes.

sage advice

Caramelizing onions cooks them to a rich brown color and an intensified sweetness. This process takes time to dissolve the strong sulfur compounds, so don't try to rush it or you'll end up with browned onions instead of richly flavored caramelized ones that are as sweet as sugar. To caramelize onions, cut the onions into thin slices. Heat 2 tablespoons olive oil or butter per onion in a large skillet over medium heat. Add the onions, and cook 25 to 30 minutes, stirring often, or until deep golden brown. Sweet onions take longer to caramelize than other varieties due to their higher moisture content.

CLASSIC PARMESAN SCALLOPED POTATOES

If it's a special occasion at our house, we almost always have scalloped potatoes. I like to play with different kinds of cheeses, but I come back to Parmesan over and over again. Use a mandoline to make easy slicing of the potatoes.

MAKES 8 TO 10 SERVINGS   **HANDS-ON 20 MINUTES**   **TOTAL 1 HOUR, 15 MINUTES**

2 lb. Yukon gold potatoes, peeled and thinly sliced
3 cups whipping cream
¼ cup chopped fresh flat-leaf parsley
2 garlic cloves, chopped
1½ tsp. table salt
¼ tsp. freshly ground black pepper
½ cup grated Parmesan cheese

1. Preheat oven to 400°F. Layer potatoes in a 13- x 9-inch or 3-quart baking dish.

2. Stir together cream and next 4 ingredients in a large bowl. Pour cream mixture over potatoes.

3. Bake at 400°F for 30 minutes, stirring gently every 10 minutes. Sprinkle with cheese; bake 15 to 20 more minutes or until bubbly and golden brown. Let stand on a wire rack 10 minutes before serving.

NEW POTATOES SMASHED AND HERBED

This crispy-on-the-outside, fluffy-on-the-inside spin on salty baked potatoes is sure to not disappoint. Grilled steak has never had a more perfect partner.

MAKES 6 SERVINGS   HANDS-ON 13 MINUTES   TOTAL 56 MINUTES

28 oz. baby red potatoes
2 tsp. kosher salt, divided
2 Tbsp. extra virgin olive oil
1 Tbsp. chopped fresh herbs
    (I used rosemary, thyme,
    and oregano)
⅛ tsp. freshly ground black
    pepper
3 Tbsp. finely grated
    Parmigiano-Reggiano cheese
    (I used a Microplane)

1. Preheat oven to 425°F. Bring potatoes, 1 teaspoon salt, and water to cover to a simmer in a Dutch oven. Reduce heat, and simmer for 15 minutes or just until fork-tender. Remove potatoes from water; place on a jelly-roll pan. Use a meat mallet to gently press each potato to ¾-inch thickness. Coat smashed potatoes with olive oil, being careful not to break up potatoes. Combine remaining 1 teaspoon salt, herbs, pepper, and cheese; set aside.

2. Roast potatoes at 425°F for 20 minutes. Carefully turn potatoes over and move them all to the center of the pan. While potatoes are crowded in the center, sprinkle with herb mixture. Move the potatoes out to evenly space them around the pan, and return to the oven for 8 minutes. Serve immediately.

sage advice

Many Southern cooks call sprouts on potatoes "eyes." They are thought to have gotten the name since they look vaguely like an eye and eyebrow thanks to a tiny leaf and bud.

CARAMELIZED ONION-
MASHED POTATO
BAKE, PAGE 123

CLASSIC PARMESAN
SCALLOPED POTATOES,
PAGE 124

NEW POTATOES SMASHED AND HERBED, PAGE 125

PICNIC POTATO SALAD

My grandmother would never have made potato salad without sweet pickle relish. Combined with grated egg and sweet onion, this classic version will never go out of style. It can be made the day before, so it's perfect for busy summer afternoons.

MAKES 8 SERVINGS   HANDS-ON 20 MINUTES   TOTAL 1 HOUR, 15 MINUTES

4 lb. Yukon gold potatoes

3 hard-cooked eggs, peeled and grated

1 cup mayonnaise

½ cup diced celery

½ cup sour cream

⅓ cup finely chopped sweet onion

¼ cup sweet pickle relish

1 Tbsp. spicy brown mustard

1 tsp. table salt

¾ tsp. freshly ground black pepper

Garnish: chopped fresh chives

1. Cook potatoes in boiling water to cover 40 minutes or until tender; drain and cool 15 minutes. Peel potatoes, and cut into 1-inch cubes.

2. Combine potatoes and eggs.

3. Stir together mayonnaise and next 7 ingredients; gently stir into potato mixture. Serve immediately, or cover and chill 12 hours.

Okra

Okra is a favorite on Southern tables. The tall, spindly plants thrive in the scorching hot summer weather and produce a pod that's ideal for frying, grilling, and pickling. Sometimes it seems the plants grow right before our eyes, and since the pods grow just as fast as the plants, most gardeners know that they need to be picked daily. It's best to pick the pods when they're no longer than 4 inches.

Many Southerners grew up with boiled okra with slime to rival a very healthy slug. A general rule to cut down on the slime is to cook it quickly and cook it hot—the longer okra cooks, the more slime will shine.

If buying okra, keep it in a paper bag in the refrigerator for up to three days.

FRESH OKRA AND TOMATOES

Okra and ripe-off-the-vine tomatoes topped with bacon are a must-have for summertime suppers. Be patient when making the roux; a roux with a nice caramel color will add a rich nutty taste that you'll love.

MAKES 4 SERVINGS   HANDS-ON 15 MINUTES   TOTAL 40 MINUTES

8 bacon slices
3 Tbsp. all-purpose flour
4 cups sliced okra (1 lb.)
¾ cup chopped onion
2 garlic cloves, minced
3 cups chopped tomato
½ tsp. table salt
½ tsp. freshly ground black pepper
¼ tsp. ground red pepper

1. Cook bacon in a large skillet over medium heat until crisp. Remove bacon, reserving 3 tablespoons drippings in skillet; discard remaining drippings. Crumble bacon, and set aside.

2. Stir flour into reserved bacon drippings, and cook over medium heat, stirring constantly, until roux is caramel colored (10 to 15 minutes).

3. Add okra, onion, and garlic; cook 2 minutes, stirring constantly. Stir in tomato and next 3 ingredients. Simmer, covered, 15 to 20 minutes or until okra is tender, stirring occasionally. Sprinkle with reserved crumbled bacon.

CAROLINA CRAB AND SHRIMP PILAU

When I think of okra, I think of my friend Virginia Willis's pilau. Each spoonful is bursting with okra and simply tastes of summertime. It's a comforting dish and gives a taste of the coast, no matter where you are. If you have shrimp or fish stock, try using it instead of the water.

MAKES 6 SERVINGS   **HANDS-ON 20 MINUTES**   **TOTAL 45 MINUTES**

1 Tbsp. canola oil
1 onion, chopped
2 garlic cloves, minced
½ lb. okra, stem ends trimmed,
    cut into ½-inch pieces
½ red bell pepper, seeded and
    diced
½ tsp. Old Bay seasoning
½ tsp. ground red pepper
1½ cups long-grain white rice
Table salt
Freshly ground black pepper
1 fresh thyme sprig
8 oz. fresh jumbo lump
    crabmeat, drained
1 lb. large raw shrimp, peeled
    and deveined

1. Heat oil in a large skillet over medium-high heat until shimmering. Add onion and cook until translucent, 2 to 5 minutes. Add garlic; cook 1 minute, stirring constantly. Add okra and bell pepper; cook until bright, another 2 minutes.

2. Add the Old Bay, ground red pepper, and rice; stir to combine. Cook, stirring constantly, until rice is coated and lightly toasted. Add salt and pepper to taste. Add 2½ cups water and thyme sprig, and stir to combine. Bring to a boil over medium-high heat. Reduce heat to simmer. Cook, covered, for 15 minutes.

3. Pick crabmeat, removing any bits of shell. Add shrimp and crabmeat, and stir to combine. Cook 5 more minutes.

4. Remove from heat, and let stand, covered, for about 5 minutes. Remove thyme sprig. Season with salt and pepper. Serve immediately.

PICKLED OKRA

At the rate okra grows, it's best to have a plan for all the extra pods, like pickling. You'll be glad you did months later when you have a tangy and slightly spicy addition to a bloody Mary or pimiento cheese sandwich.

MAKES 7 (1-PINT) JARS   HANDS-ON 40 MINUTES   TOTAL 12 HOURS, 40 MINUTES

1 (9-piece) canning kit,
   including canner, jar lifter,
   and canning rack
7 (1-pt.) canning jars
2½ lb. small fresh okra
7 small fresh green or red chile
   peppers
7 garlic cloves
2 Tbsp. plus 1 tsp. dill seeds
4 cups white vinegar
   (5% acidity)
½ cup table salt
¼ cup sugar

1. Bring canner half-full with water to a boil; simmer. Meanwhile, place jars in a large stockpot with water to cover; bring to a boil, and simmer. Place bands and lids in a large saucepan with water to cover; bring to a boil, and simmer. Remove hot jars, 1 at a time, using jar lifter.

2. Pack okra into hot jars, filling to ½ inch from top. Place 1 pepper, 1 garlic clove, and 1 teaspoon dill seeds in each jar. Bring vinegar, salt, sugar, and 4 cups water to a boil over medium-high heat. Pour over okra, filling to ½ inch from top.

3. Wipe jar rims; cover at once with metal lids, and screw on bands (snug but not too tight). Place jars in canning rack, and place in simmering water in canner. Add additional boiling water as needed to cover by 1 to 2 inches.

4. Bring water to a rolling boil; boil 10 minutes. Remove from heat. Cool jars in canner 5 minutes. Transfer jars to a cutting board; cool 12 to 24 hours. Test seals of jars by pressing center of each lid. If lids do not pop, jars are properly sealed. (See page 139 for more information.) Store in a cool, dry place at room temperature up to 1 year.

SMASHED FRIED OKRA

Having a crispier surface to enjoy on the okra is nothing short of brilliant. A smack with a meat mallet makes each pod "blossom" for the best frying possible. Try serving the crunchy pods with a dipping sauce, like rémoulade.

MAKES 4 TO 6 SERVINGS   HANDS-ON 40 MINUTES   TOTAL 40 MINUTES

1 lb. fresh okra
1½ cups buttermilk
2 cups plain yellow cornmeal
Kosher salt
Freshly ground black pepper
Canola oil

1. Use a meat mallet to smash okra, starting at tip of pod and working toward stem end. Place buttermilk in a shallow dish, and place cornmeal in another shallow dish. Stir desired amount of salt and pepper into buttermilk and cornmeal. Dip okra in buttermilk; dredge in cornmeal, shaking off excess.

2. Pour oil to depth of 2 inches into a large Dutch oven; heat to 350°F. Fry okra, in batches, 2 to 3 minutes or until browned and crisp, turning once. Remove okra, using a slotted spoon; drain on paper towels. Add salt and pepper to taste; serve immediately.

CANNING IN A HURRY

Cooks who know the season is short and the peak is precious are those who can. Making preserves and chutneys to savor the flavor a little longer is a bit of a Southern rite of passage. Before the days of refrigeration, processing canned goods was a necessity for any shelf life beyond a few days. As traditional as processing jars and waiting on the lids to seal is, it's not for everyone. With busier schedules and a lack of canning equipment, quick canning has become much more popular. Thanks to the convenience of refrigerators, we can skip the processing and keep everything chilled.

Begin with the freshest produce possible. Use glass jars for any homemade jam, relish, or preserve, just as you would if you were going through processing, add the lid, and simply refrigerate them. Label and date the jars so you remember the date of the batch. They won't last as long as those that have been processed, but it's a fast way to a very rewarding finish.

A THREE-STEP GUIDE TO PUTTIN' UP

To get started, you'll need a basic canner, a jar lifter, and a canning rack.

Step 1: Sterilize. Bring a canner half full of water to a boil; simmer. Place jars in a large stockpot with water to cover; bring to a boil, and simmer 10 minutes. Place bands and lids in a large saucepan. (Always use new lids.) Cover bands and lids with hot water from canner to soften gaskets. Let stand 10 minutes.

Step 2: Prepare Recipe. Remove hot jars from stockpot, 1 at a time, using jar lifter, and fill as directed in chosen recipe.

Step 3: Seal & Process. Wipe rims of filled jars. Cover at once with metal lids, and screw on bands (snug but not too tight). Place jars in canning rack, and place in canner. Add more boiling water as needed to cover jars by 1 to 2 inches. Bring to a rolling boil; boil 15 minutes, adjusting time for altitude.* Turn off heat, and let stand 5 minutes. Remove jars, and let stand at room temperature 24 hours. Test seals of jars by pressing centers of lids. If lids do not pop, jars are properly sealed. If the lids pop, refrigerate immediately and use contents within a few days. Store in a cool, dark place at room temperature up to 1 year. Refrigerate after opening.

*Consult the USDA Complete Guide to Home Canning at nchfp.uga.edu/publications/publications_usda.html to adjust processing times for altitude.

Peppers

There's a pepper for any liking—sweet bell peppers, hot jalapeños, spicy chile peppers, and the list could go on for a day.

Look for peppers that are glossy and firm. If using them the same day, store them at room temperature. They'll keep in paper bags in the refrigerator for up to a week. If peppers are kept just a little too long and become soft, it doesn't affect the flavor, just the texture. Green bell peppers are underripe and have a slightly sour taste. A yellow bell pepper, my favorite, has the mildest flavor.

HOT PEPPER SAUCE

Field peas and greens just aren't the same without a splash of this tangy hot sauce. Store it in the refrigerator and as the vinegar runs low, simply add more. It's been said that no respectable Southern kitchen is without one of these beautiful bottles.

**MAKES ABOUT 1¾ CUPS   HANDS-ON 10 MINUTES
TOTAL 20 MINUTES, PLUS 3 WEEKS FOR CHILLING**

1 cup red and green Thai chile
   peppers, stemmed
1 cup apple cider vinegar
1 tsp. table salt
1 tsp. sugar

1. Fill 1 (14-ounce) glass jar with red and green Thai chile peppers, filling to about 1 inch from top of jar.

2. Bring vinegar, salt, and sugar to a boil in a small saucepan over medium heat, stirring until salt and sugar are dissolved (about 2 to 3 minutes). Remove from heat, and let stand 5 minutes. Pour hot mixture over peppers in jar. Cover and chill 3 weeks. Store in refrigerator up to 6 months.

NOTE: Chilling for 3 weeks allows the peppers to fire up the vinegar mixture. The longer it sits, the spicier it becomes. Remember to wear rubber gloves when working with peppers.

put 'em up

To dry small peppers, like tabasco or serrano, string them in the kitchen. Use a sewing needle and thread to string the peppers through the stems. Tie a loop at each end of the thread to hang horizontally. If hanging vertically, tie knots in between the peppers to keep the peppers separated. Allow to dry until shriveled and crispy, about a month. Store in an airtight container for up to one year. Grind peppers for dried pepper flakes, or crush and add to salsas and sauces.

FANCY PIMIENTO CHEESE

This is quite possibly the most beautiful version of pimiento cheese I've made—and I've made a lot of the Southern delicacy. It's pretty enough for a cracker and creamy enough for the softest white bread. Roasting peppers and skipping the jarred versions really makes a difference.

MAKES 4 CUPS   HANDS-ON 18 MINUTES   TOTAL 36 MINUTES

1 red bell pepper

1 orange bell pepper

1 (10-oz.) block extra-sharp white Cheddar cheese

1 (10-oz.) block extra-sharp Cheddar cheese

½ cup chopped pecans, toasted

4 green onions, sliced

½ jalapeño pepper, seeded and minced

3 Tbsp. chopped fresh flat-leaf parsley

⅓ cup mayonnaise

1 Tbsp. dill pickle juice

1. Preheat broiler to high. Cut bell peppers in half lengthwise; discard seeds and membranes. Place, skin sides up, on a foil-lined baking sheet; flatten with hand. Broil 8 minutes or until blackened. Wrap bell peppers in foil; let stand 10 minutes. Remove and discard peel; finely chop peppers.

2. Shred cheeses on a box grater; transfer to large bowl. Stir in bell peppers and remaining ingredients. Chill until serving. Store, covered, in refrigerator up to 1 week.

NOTE: I tested with Cracker Barrel Cheddar Cheese.

PEPPER JACK GRITS POPPERS

The classic bar snack is dressed up with grits to start any meal off right. Look for mini bell peppers in a range of colors for the prettiest presentation. For extra fun, enjoy these little delights with a glass of Champagne.

MAKES 10 APPETIZER SERVINGS **HANDS-ON 35 MINUTES**
TOTAL 8 HOURS, 40 MINUTES

1 cup hot cooked grits

1 cup (4 oz.) freshly shredded
   pepper Jack cheese

½ cup shredded Parmesan
   cheese

2 Tbsp. chopped fresh cilantro

1 garlic clove, pressed

18 to 20 sweet mini bell
   peppers

1. Stir together first 5 ingredients until cheese is melted; add salt and pepper to taste. Cover and chill 8 hours.

2. Preheat broiler with oven rack 6 inches from heat. Cut peppers in half lengthwise, leaving stems intact; remove seeds. Spoon grits mixture into pepper halves. Place on a broiler pan. Broil 4 minutes or until golden.

sage advice

Chilling grits gives any leftovers a second life. Once they're solidified, they can be cut or shaped and heated quickly at high heat in the oven or on the grill. It's a good reason to make more than you need for breakfast.

SERRANO PEPPER BURGERS

This burger has a perfect combination of smoky heat with a little sweetness. The grilled serrano peppers, melted pepper Jack cheese, and all the toppings are a good reason to fire up the grill.

MAKES 12 SERVINGS   HANDS-ON 45 MINUTES   TOTAL 1 HOUR

1 lb. serrano peppers
2 Tbsp. olive oil
Kosher salt
3 lb. ground chuck
Freshly ground black pepper
1 lb. pepper Jack cheese,
    thinly sliced
Butter
12 hamburger buns
Toppings: mayonnaise,
    ketchup, mustard, lettuce,
    tomato slices

1. Light 1 side of grill, heating to 350° to 400°F (medium-high) heat; leave other side unlit. Toss together peppers and olive oil. Arrange peppers in a grill basket or on an aluminum-foil tray over unlit side, and grill, covered with grill lid, 10 to 15 minutes or until peppers begin to shrivel. Transfer peppers to lit side of grill, and grill, covered with grill lid, 8 to 10 minutes or until lightly charred, turning halfway through. Remove from grill to a wire rack, and cool completely (about 15 minutes).

2. Remove and discard stems; slice peppers in half lengthwise. Remove seeds, and sprinkle peppers with desired amount of salt.

3. Preheat both sides of grill to 350° to 400°F (medium-high) heat. Shape ground chuck into 12 patties; sprinkle with desired amount of salt and pepper. Grill patties, without grill lid, 4 to 5 minutes on each side or to desired degree of doneness. Place 2 to 3 pepper halves on each patty; top with cheese. Grill, covered with grill lid, 1 to 2 minutes or until cheese melts.

4. Butter buns, and toast on grill. Serve patties on toasted buns with desired toppings.

Summer Squash

Zucchini and yellow squash are proud plants that produce with abundance. There is a fine line of when the squash is too unripe to eat and when it's gone too far. The larger the squash, the more fibrous it is. And as fast as it grows, that line is one that passes in the blink of an eye.

In the market, look for brightly colored, firm squashes that are heavy for their size. The taste of smaller squash is better than larger ones. Bruises and dents should be avoided if possible because they can speed decay. No need to peel the squash. The skins are thin, tasty, and packed with nutrients.

Don't pass on the beautiful squash and zucchini blossoms. Stuff them, fry them, or sauté them for a stunning and delicate treat.

QUICK BUTTERED PATTYPAN SQUASH WITH DILL

My children call pattypans little UFOs. They are a top-shaped squash variety known for their beauty. Younger pattypans are more tender, so look for baby versions, or use baby crookneck squash or zucchini.

MAKES 6 SERVINGS   **HANDS-ON 23 MINUTES**   **TOTAL 23 MINUTES**

1½ lb. baby pattypan squash

3 Tbsp. unsalted butter

1 cup sliced shallots

½ tsp. table salt

¼ tsp. freshly ground black
　pepper

¼ cup firmly packed fresh dill,
　torn into pieces

1. Remove stems from squash, and cut each squash into fourths.

2. Heat butter in a large skillet over medium heat. Add shallots, and cook for 3 minutes or until beginning to brown. Add squash, salt, and pepper. Cook, stirring often, for 10 to 12 minutes or until lightly browned and tender. Transfer squash to a serving plate, and sprinkle with dill.

put 'em up

Squash and zucchini make excellent pickles. When the crop is exploding, slice them thinly and pickle away for later. (Try the Spicy Icebox Pickles on page 99.) I like to add fresh dill to jars to complement the squash.

NATHALIE'S CHICKEN STUFFED UNDER THE SKIN

Nathalie Dupree has filled a lot of roles in my life. She's been a mentor, friend, teacher, confidant, and many others. I apprenticed with her when I was in college. I knew very little about cooking, and she paved the road for me on the journey of a lifetime. One of the first recipes I cooked in her kitchen was her chicken stuffed with zucchini. She was inspired by Richard Olney's original version of the recipe, and the inspiration was then passed on to me. Ask your butcher to remove the backbone and flatten the chicken, called spatchcocking, to help you save time.

MAKES 4 SERVINGS   HANDS-ON 1 HOUR, 30 MINUTES   TOTAL 3 HOURS

1 lb. zucchini

3 Tbsp. unsalted butter

1 yellow onion, chopped

3 oz. cream cheese, softened

⅓ cup unsalted butter, softened

1 cup freshly grated
   Parmigiano-Reggiano cheese

1 large egg, beaten

¼ cup chopped fresh herbs
   (I used parsley, thyme,
   rosemary, and oregano)

1 tsp. table salt, divided

1 tsp. freshly ground black
   pepper, divided

1 (3½-lb.) whole chicken

1. Preheat oven to 375°F.

2. Grate unpeeled zucchini on the large holes of a box grater or in a food processor fitted with the grater blade. Heat 3 tablespoons butter in a large skillet over medium-low heat. Add onion and cook until soft. Add zucchini and cook 4 to 5 minutes, stirring often. Cool; set aside.

3. Combine cream cheese, butter, next 3 ingredients, and ½ teaspoon salt and ½ teaspoon pepper. Stir in zucchini mixture.

4. Remove the backbone of the chicken by cutting from tail to neck on either side of the spine. Place chicken breast side up; press breastbone to flatten slightly.

5. Keeping skin intact, loosen between skin and meat of entire bird with fingers. Stuff the chicken, forcing a small handful of stuffing at a time, under the skin of the breast first, then the thighs, and drumsticks, if possible.

6. When completely stuffed, mixture under skin will be thick and will ooze in a few places. Carefully place chicken in a roasting pan, sprinkling with remaining ½ teaspoon salt and pepper. Roast at 375°F for 1½ hours, basting frequently. Allow to rest 15 minutes before serving.

SQUASH CASSEROLE

It's hard to grow up in the South and not fall in love with squash casserole. No potluck or family gathering should be without it on the table. The French fried onions make this one extra memorable.

MAKES 8 TO 10 SERVINGS   **HANDS-ON 40 MINUTES**   **TOTAL 1 HOUR, 15 MINUTES**

4 lb. yellow squash, sliced

1 large sweet onion, finely chopped

1 cup (4 oz.) freshly shredded Cheddar cheese

1 cup mayonnaise

2 Tbsp. chopped fresh basil

1 tsp. garlic salt

1 tsp. freshly ground black pepper

2 large eggs, lightly beaten

2 cups soft, fresh breadcrumbs, divided

1¼ cups (5 oz.) freshly shredded Parmesan cheese, divided

2 Tbsp. butter, melted

½ cup crushed French fried onions

1. Preheat oven to 350°F. Cook yellow squash and sweet onion in boiling water to cover in a Dutch oven 8 minutes or just until vegetables are tender; drain squash mixture well.

2. Combine squash mixture, freshly shredded Cheddar cheese, next 5 ingredients, 1 cup breadcrumbs, and ¾ cup Parmesan cheese. Spoon into a lightly greased 13- x 9-inch baking dish.

3. Stir together melted butter, French fried onions, and remaining 1 cup breadcrumbs and ½ cup Parmesan cheese. Sprinkle over squash mixture.

4. Bake at 350°F for 35 to 40 minutes or until set.

CHOCOLATE ZUCCHINI CAKES

Chocolate and vegetables should pair up more often! Fresh zucchini makes these little cakes incredibly moist. The frosting sets up quickly, so make it after the cakes are completely cooled.

MAKES 6 CAKES   HANDS-ON 30 MINUTES   TOTAL 2 HOURS, 45 MINUTES

2 cups sugar

½ cup butter, softened

½ cup canola oil

3 large eggs

2⅓ cups all-purpose flour

⅔ cup unsweetened cocoa

1 tsp. baking soda

1 tsp. table salt

½ tsp. ground cinnamon

⅔ cup whole buttermilk

2 cups grated unpeeled
   zucchini (about 2 medium)

1 (4-oz.) semisweet chocolate
   baking bar, finely chopped

2 tsp. vanilla extract

6 (5- x 3-inch) disposable
   aluminum foil loaf pans,
   lightly greased

Chocolate Fudge Frosting

1. Preheat oven to 350°F. Beat first 3 ingredients at medium speed with a heavy-duty electric stand mixer until light and fluffy. Add eggs, 1 at a time, beating just until blended after each addition. Sift together flour and next 4 ingredients; add to butter mixture alternately with buttermilk, beginning and ending with flour mixture. Beat at low speed just until blended after each addition. Stir zucchini and next 2 ingredients into batter. Spoon batter into 6 lightly greased 5- x 3-inch loaf pans, filling two-thirds full.

2. Bake at 350°F for 30 to 35 minutes or until a wooden pick inserted in center comes out clean. Cool completely in pans on wire racks (about 1 hour).

3. Prepare Chocolate Fudge Frosting. Spoon hot frosting over cooled cakes; cool completely (about 30 minutes).

CHOCOLATE FUDGE FROSTING

**MAKES ABOUT 2 CUPS   HANDS-ON 15 MINUTES
TOTAL 15 MINUTES**

⅓ cup butter

⅓ cup unsweetened cocoa

⅓ cup milk

¼ cup sour cream

2 tsp. vanilla extract

3 cups powdered sugar

Cook first 3 ingredients in a large saucepan over medium heat, stirring constantly, 3 to 4 minutes or until butter melts. Remove from heat; whisk in sour cream and vanilla. Gradually add powdered sugar, beating at medium speed with an electric mixer until smooth. Use immediately.

Tomatoes

Quite possibly the quintessential vegetable of Southern summers, tomatoes are sacred. They originated in Peru, and although tomatoes are scientifically a fruit, the U.S. Supreme Court officially declared them a vegetable in the late 1800s.

Tomatoes come in nearly endless varieties that cover the spectrum of colors and size. The popular vegetable is produced by two different types of plants: one that grows tomatoes all summer long and one that just grows one crop. Most tomatoes found in grocery stores are hybrids that are more sturdy than delicate heirlooms. Hybrids are mass-produced with less flavor and character than heirloom varieties (see page 196). From tiny grape tomatoes to huge Mortgage Lifters, flavor and texture differ from very firm and dense to soft and run-down-your-arm juicy. It's worth an extensive taste test to find your favorite!

One of the most important rules is that they should be stored at room temperature only, *never* in the refrigerator. The closer the tomato was grown to your house, the better—the flavor of a local tomato is simply unbeatable. Once you've tasted the difference, you'll never look at store-bought tomatoes the same. A ripe tomato will smell like a tomato and it should be heavy for its size.

CUCUMBER TOMATO ASPIC

When I was small, we always had a ring of tomato aspic for Christmas with a generous dollop of mayonnaise right in the center. Some Southerners enjoy it as a side dish to the traditional roasted turkey or as a start to the meal. In more recent years, aspic has fallen slightly out of favor, as have most congealed salads. Think of it like a Bloody Mary, sans alcohol, that you can eat with a spoon.

MAKES 16 TO 20 SERVINGS   HANDS-ON 20 MINUTES
TOTAL 4 HOURS, 20 MINUTES

1 envelope unflavored gelatin

1 cup cranberry juice

3 cups low-sodium tomato juice

2 Tbsp. chopped fresh flat-leaf parsley

1 Tbsp. olive oil

1 tsp. Worcestershire sauce

6 to 8 dashes of hot sauce

½ tsp. celery salt

½ tsp. garlic salt

1¾ cups chopped cucumber

1. Sprinkle gelatin over cranberry juice in a bowl. Let stand 3 minutes.

2. Meanwhile, bring tomato juice to a boil in a medium saucepan over medium-high heat. Pour over gelatin mixture, and stir until gelatin dissolves. Whisk in parsley and next 5 ingredients.

3. Spread cucumber in a 4-cup mold; pour gelatin mixture over cucumber. Chill 4 hours or until set. Dip bottom of mold in warm water for about 15 seconds. Unmold onto a serving plate.

sage advice

Tomatoes, like oranges, contain stored up sunshine, that is when they are gathered ripe. It is the warm sunshine that develops or makes vitamins. So after years of growing and eating them, we have come to know the true value of tomatoes.

—Mrs. S.R. Dull in *Southern Cooking* (1928)

HEIRLOOM TOMATO SANDWICH BITES

Baby showers, garden clubs, and summer parties just got better with these little, bitty open-faced tomato sandwiches. If possible, use different colors of heirloom tomatoes to really make them showstopping. Don't let the tomato and bread scraps go to waste. Make a summer panzanella.

MAKES 30 SANDWICHES   HANDS-ON 15 MINUTES   TOTAL 15 MINUTES

1 cup mayonnaise

⅓ cup finely shredded Parmigiano-Reggiano cheese (I used a Microplane)

2 Tbsp. chopped fresh herbs (I used rosemary, sage, oregano, and chives)

⅛ tsp. table salt

⅛ tsp. freshly ground black pepper, plus more for garnish

1 (16-oz.) loaf very thin white bread

5 to 6 (6-oz.) heirloom tomatoes, varying in color

Garnish: fresh oregano sprigs

1. Combine mayonnaise and next 4 ingredients in a small bowl. Set aside.

2. Using a 2-inch round cutter, cut bread slices into circles, reserving trimmings for another use, if desired. Slice tomatoes into ⅓-inch-thick slices. (If tomato slices are larger than 2 inches, use the same 2-inch cutter to cut tomatoes into circles.) Generously spread mayonnaise mixture on 1 side of bread rounds. Top each with a tomato circle.

NOTE: I tested with Pepperidge Farm Very Thin White Bread.

⇝ put 'em up ⇜

Raw tomatoes don't freeze well. They can become mealy and lose flavor. Roast them before freezing them for the best results. Here's how: Stir together 4 pints cherry tomatoes, 1 tablespoon olive oil, 4 garlic cloves, 1 teaspoon salt, 1 teaspoon sugar, and 1 teaspoon freshly ground black pepper. Bake at 350°F in a single layer in a jelly-roll pan for 1 hour and 20 minutes. Remove and discard garlic. Stir in ½ cup chopped fresh basil, 2 teaspoons balsamic vinegar, and ½ teaspoon table salt.

TOMATO, CHEDDAR, AND BACON PIE

A homemade crust is the beginning to this showstopping tomato pie. Choose a variety of colors and sizes of tomatoes to add some wow. Seed and drain the slices before adding them into the crust. Be prepared to be asked for this recipe again and again.

MAKES 6 TO 8 SERVINGS   **HANDS-ON 45 MINUTES**   **TOTAL 3 HOURS**

2¼ cups self-rising soft-wheat flour (such as White Lily)

1 cup cold butter, cut up

8 cooked bacon slices, chopped

¾ cup sour cream

2¾ lb. assorted large tomatoes, divided

2 tsp. kosher salt, divided

1½ cups (6 oz.) freshly shredded extra-sharp Cheddar cheese

½ cup freshly shredded Parmigiano-Reggiano cheese

½ cup mayonnaise

1 large egg, lightly beaten

2 Tbsp. fresh dill sprigs

1 Tbsp. chopped fresh chives

1 Tbsp. chopped fresh flat-leaf parsley

1 Tbsp. apple cider vinegar

1 green onion, thinly sliced

2 tsp. sugar

¼ tsp. black pepper

1½ Tbsp. plain yellow cornmeal

Garnish: fresh basil

1. Place flour in bowl of a heavy-duty electric stand mixer; cut in cold butter with a pastry blender or fork until mixture resembles small peas. Chill 10 minutes. Add bacon to flour mixture; beat at low speed just until combined. Gradually add sour cream, ¼ cup at a time, beating just until blended after each addition.

2. Spoon mixture onto a heavily floured surface; sprinkle lightly with flour, and knead 3 or 4 times, adding more flour as needed. Roll into a 13-inch round. Gently place dough in a 9-inch fluted tart pan with 2-inch sides and a removable bottom. Press dough into pan; trim off excess dough along edges. Chill 30 minutes.

3. Meanwhile, cut 2 pounds tomatoes into ¼-inch-thick slices, and remove seeds. Place tomatoes in a single layer on paper towels; sprinkle with 1 teaspoon salt. Let stand 30 minutes.

4. Preheat oven to 425°F. Stir together Cheddar cheese, next 10 ingredients, and remaining 1 teaspoon salt in a bowl until combined.

5. Pat tomato slices dry with a paper towel. Sprinkle cornmeal over bottom of crust. Lightly spread ½ cup cheese mixture onto crust; layer with half of tomato slices in slightly overlapping rows. Spread with ½ cup cheese mixture. Repeat layers, using remaining tomato slices and cheese mixture. Cut remaining ¾ pound tomatoes into ¼-inch-thick slices; arrange on top of pie.

6. Bake at 425°F for 40 to 45 minutes, shielding edges with foil during last 20 minutes to prevent excessive browning. Let stand 1 to 2 hours before serving.

TOMATO, CHEDDAR,
AND BACON PIE,
PAGE 159

HEIRLOOM TOMATO
SANDWICH BITES,
PAGE 158

BLT BENEDICT WITH AVOCADO-TOMATO RELISH

From a woman who got married in the morning for the sole purpose of celebrating over breakfast, you can trust that this is a recipe worthy of rave reviews. A soft poached egg creates the effect of traditional hollandaise over the open-faced sandwich.

MAKES 6 SERVINGS   **HANDS-ON 23 MINUTES**   **TOTAL 23 MINUTES**

1 cup halved grape tomatoes

1 avocado, diced

1 Tbsp. chopped fresh basil

1 garlic clove, minced

2 Tbsp. extra virgin olive oil

1 Tbsp. red wine vinegar, divided

6 large eggs

¼ cup mayonnaise

6 (¾-inch-thick) bakery bread slices, toasted

3 cups firmly packed arugula

12 thick bacon slices, cooked

1. Combine tomatoes, next 4 ingredients, and 2½ teaspoons red wine vinegar in a small bowl.

2. Add water to depth of 3 inches in a large saucepan. Bring to a boil; reduce heat, and maintain at a light simmer. Add remaining ½ teaspoon red wine vinegar. Break eggs, and slip into water, 1 at a time, as close as possible to surface. Simmer 3 to 5 minutes or to desired degree of doneness. Remove with a slotted spoon. Trim edges, if desired.

3. Spread mayonnaise on 1 side of each bread slice. Layer each with ½ cup arugula, 2 bacon slices, and 1 egg. Top with tomato mixture.

⟫⟫ *put 'em up* ⟪⟪

When the tomatoes are coming in by the armfuls, show them off with a sweet jam. I love to serve this Easy Tomato Jam with field peas and hot pepper sauce. Simmer 4 pounds peeled, seeded, and chopped tomatoes, 1 cup sugar, 2 tablespoons orange zest, ⅔ cup orange juice, 2 teaspoons lemon zest, 1 tablespoon lemon juice, ½ teaspoon dried crushed red pepper, and ¼ teaspoon kosher salt in a large saucepan over medium-low heat, stirring occasionally, 1 hour. Cool, cover, and chill. Makes 6 servings.

FRIED GREEN TOMATOES

When I have friends visit who have never been to the South, one of their first requests to eat is fried green tomatoes. Green tomatoes are picked before they ripen to red. At this stage, they are very firm and slightly sour. Buttermilk, cornmeal, and salt are the keys to this classic.

MAKES 4 TO 6 SERVINGS   HANDS-ON 35 MINUTES   TOTAL 35 MINUTES

1 large egg, lightly beaten

½ cup buttermilk

½ cup all-purpose flour, divided

½ cup plain yellow cornmeal

1 tsp. table salt

½ tsp. freshly ground black pepper

3 medium-size green tomatoes, cut into ⅓-inch slices

Vegetable oil

1. Combine egg and buttermilk; set aside.

2. Combine ¼ cup all-purpose flour, cornmeal, 1 teaspoon salt, and pepper in a shallow bowl or pan.

3. Dredge tomato slices in remaining ¼ cup flour; dip in egg mixture, and dredge in cornmeal mixture, shaking off excess.

4. Pour oil to depth of ¼ to ½ inch in a large cast-iron skillet; heat to 375°F. Fry tomatoes, in batches, in hot oil 2 minutes on each side or until golden. Drain on paper towels or a rack. Sprinkle hot tomatoes with salt.

sage advice

There is nothing better you can do with a homegrown tomato than to eat it out of hand, sitting on the porch and spinning dreams into a Southern night.

—Ronni Lundy in *Butter Beans to Blackberries* (North Point Press, 1999)

Fall

Fall vegetables offer deeper flavors and richer textures
in earthy shades of yellow, orange, purple, green, and brown.
The foods are heartier, warming us from the inside out.

Broccoli & Cauliflower

Broccoli and cauliflower are in the same genus and species but are not in the same cultivar. These bunches of unopened flowers are delicate and should be eaten within a day or two from purchase.

Avoid heads that are bruised. The tighter the florets are gathered, the fresher the vegetable. The stems and the leaves of both cauliflower and broccoli are often overlooked but are very edible. Peel the stems as needed to remove the fibrous outer skin, and add them to soups or enjoy them raw. Sauté the tender leaves with a little butter and salt. Both the color and the taste of the florets will benefit from shorter heat times.

Store the vegetables stem side up so water doesn't collect on the head. Keep in an open bag for up to one week in the refrigerator.

BROCCOLI, GRAPE, AND PASTA SALAD

Grape and broccoli salads have long been on Southern luncheon menus. Bacon, pasta, and a tangy-sweet dressing make this a version you'll serve over and over.

MAKES 6 TO 8 SERVINGS   HANDS-ON 25 MINUTES   TOTAL 3 HOURS, 30 MINUTES

½ (16-oz.) package farfalle (bow-tie) pasta

1 lb. fresh broccoli

1 cup mayonnaise

⅓ cup sugar

⅓ cup diced red onion

⅓ cup red wine vinegar

1 tsp. table salt

2 cups seedless red grapes, halved

8 thick bacon slices, cooked and crumbled

1 cup toasted chopped pecans

1. Prepare pasta according to package directions.

2. Meanwhile, cut broccoli florets from stems, and separate florets into small pieces using tip of a paring knife. Peel away tough outer layer of stems, and finely chop stems.

3. Whisk together mayonnaise and next 4 ingredients in a large bowl; add broccoli, hot cooked pasta, and grapes, and stir to coat. Cover and chill 3 hours. Stir bacon and pecans into salad just before serving.

BROCCOLI WITH PIMIENTO CHEESE SAUCE

Broccoli has been smothered in cheese for ages, but this Pimiento Cheese Sauce dresses it up for the better! Fresh breadcrumbs add just enough crunch to take it over the top.

**MAKES 6 TO 8 SERVINGS   HANDS-ON 17 MINUTES
TOTAL 33 MINUTES, INCLUDING MAKING PIMIENTO CHEESE SAUCE**

2 lb. fresh broccoli, cut into
   spears
Pimiento Cheese Sauce
1 cup soft white breadcrumbs
2 Tbsp. butter, melted
⅓ cup shredded Parmesan
   cheese

1. Preheat oven to 375°F. Arrange broccoli in a steamer basket over boiling water. Cover and steam 5 minutes or just until crisp-tender.

2. Arrange broccoli in a lightly greased 11- x 7-inch baking dish. Pour Pimiento Cheese Sauce evenly over broccoli.

3. Combine breadcrumbs, melted butter, and cheese; sprinkle evenly over cheese sauce.

4. Bake at 375°F for 20 minutes or until thoroughly heated.

PIMIENTO CHEESE SAUCE

MAKES 3½ CUPS   HANDS-ON 16 MINUTES   TOTAL 16 MINUTES

¼ cup butter
¼ cup all-purpose flour
2 cups milk
¼ tsp. table salt
1 tsp. Worcestershire sauce

2 cups (8 oz.) shredded sharp
   Cheddar cheese
1 (4-oz.) jar diced pimiento,
   drained

1. Melt butter in a heavy saucepan over medium heat; add flour, stirring until smooth. Cook, stirring constantly, 1 minute.

2. Add milk gradually; cook, stirring constantly, until mixture is thickened and bubbly. Stir in salt and remaining ingredients.

KALAMATA CAULIFLOWER AND CRISPY CAPERS

My little girl, Adair, can't get enough roasted cauliflower. When I make it, she eats it like candy. This pan-roasted version is faster than cooking in the oven. The saltiness of olives and capers varies greatly, so make sure to taste for salt before serving.

MAKES 4 SERVINGS   HANDS-ON 25 MINUTES   TOTAL 25 MINUTES

¼ cup olive oil

3 Tbsp. capers, drained

1 large head cauliflower,
   cut into small florets
   (8 cups florets)

2 garlic cloves, minced

¼ cup pitted kalamata olives,
   chopped

1 lemon, cut into 4 wedges

1. Heat ¼ cup olive oil in a large skillet over medium heat. Add capers and cook 4 to 5 minutes, shaking skillet often, until capers are crispy. Remove capers from oil, and drain on paper towels.

2. Reserving oil in skillet, add cauliflower florets, and add table salt and black pepper to taste. Toss skillet to coat cauliflower in oil, and cook 15 minutes, stirring often, until deeply browned and fork-tender. Add garlic and olives; cook 3 minutes. Remove from skillet to a platter, and sprinkle with capers. Serve with lemon wedges.

sage advice

Look for pitted olives when choosing kalamatas at the grocery store.
It saves time and makes a stubborn apron stain much less likely.

BROWNED BUTTER CAULIFLOWER MASH

Browned butter adds an autumn-like nuttiness to this alternative to mashed potatoes. It's an easy-to-pair side dish that you'll make again and again.

MAKES 6 SERVINGS   HANDS-ON 13 MINUTES   TOTAL 20 MINUTES

1 head medium cauliflower
   (about 2 lb.), chopped*
½ cup sour cream
¾ tsp. table salt
½ tsp. freshly ground black
   pepper
¼ cup grated Parmesan cheese
1 Tbsp. chopped fresh chives
2 Tbsp. butter
Garnish: fresh chives

1. Pour water to a depth of ¼ inch into a large Dutch oven. Arrange cauliflower in Dutch oven. Cook, covered, over medium-high heat 7 to 10 minutes or until tender. Drain.

2. Process cauliflower, sour cream, salt, and pepper in a food processor 30 seconds or until smooth, stopping to scrape down sides as needed. Stir in cheese and chives. Place in a bowl.

3. If desired, microwave mixture at HIGH 1 to 2 minutes or until thoroughly heated, stirring at 1-minute intervals.

4. Cook butter in a small heavy saucepan over medium heat, stirring constantly, 4 to 5 minutes or until butter begins to turn golden brown. Remove from heat, and immediately drizzle butter over cauliflower mixture. Serve immediately.

*2 (16-ounce) bags frozen cauliflower may be substituted. Cook cauliflower according to package directions. Proceed with recipe as directed, beginning with Step 2.

Jerusalem Artichokes

Depending on where in the South you live, these elusive vegetables are adored and desired or simply are unknown and unappreciated. I had never heard of one until I moved to Charleston, South Carolina. In the Lowcountry, the tubers of the sunflower plant have quite the following. When sunflower season is over, cut down the stalks and dig up the underground goodies. Some call them sunchokes and others just artichokes. They are in the same family as the artichoke, but that's the only resemblance.

The lumpy tuber looks similar to ginger and is loaded with vitamins, fiber, and calcium. Once out of the ground, the shelf life is short so only dig as much as you can cook that day. Many make their way into a famous Lowcountry condiment of pickles or relish.

They shouldn't be soft or damp or have any sprouts. Store them in the refrigerator in an open bag up to three days. Peeling isn't necessary. Trim away any dark spots on the flesh. They should be firm and not spongy when purchased. One quirk of the Lowcountry favorite is they don't cook evenly. You'll always have a few overcooked and some underdone.

JERUSALEM ARTICHOKES ROASTED WITH LEMONS

Try to choose smaller artichokes for the most tender textures. Roasting the tubers brings out their earthy and savory nutty flavors. Be patient and stir only twice for maximum browning and crispy edges.

MAKES 4 SERVINGS   HANDS-ON 10 MINUTES   TOTAL 55 MINUTES

1½ lb. Jerusalem artichokes
2 shallots
4 sprigs fresh rosemary
5 Tbsp. extra virgin olive oil, divided
¾ tsp. table salt
½ tsp. freshly ground black pepper
1 lemon, cut into 4 wedges

1. Preheat oven to 450°F.

2. Wash and scrub Jerusalem artichokes well. Pat dry; cut into 1-inch pieces. Peel and cut shallots lengthwise into quarters, maintaining the core to keep together. Combine artichokes, shallots, and rosemary in a medium bowl. Add ¼ cup olive oil, tossing to coat well.

3. Arrange artichoke mixture in a single layer on a jelly-roll pan. Sprinkle with salt and pepper. Toss lemon wedges with remaining 1 tablespoon olive oil. Arrange lemon wedges on pan.

4. Roast at 450°F for 15 minutes. Gently stir to turn artichoke slices, leaving the lemon slices undisturbed. Roast 20 more minutes, then stir again. Roast a final 10 minutes.

5. Remove the woody rosemary stems before serving. Serve with roasted lemon wedges for squeezing over artichokes.

sage advice

A handheld vegetable brush makes scrubbing hard vegetables, like potatoes and Jerusalem artichokes, easy. There's no need for soap. It takes just a little elbow grease to remove any clinging soil.

JERUSALEM ARTICHOKE PICKLE RELISH

A staple in Lowcountry pantries, this tart and tangy relish is both unique and sought after. It's a popular condiment on Southern coastal Thanksgiving tables. Families are known to pass down their recipes to their children to carry on the relish-canning tradition. There is an ongoing debate on the addition of bell peppers and other vegetables to the relish. I've chosen the less controversial position of just adding onions. Wear an apron—turmeric has powerful staining ability.

MAKES 5 (1-PINT) JARS   HANDS-ON 1 HOUR   TOTAL 1 HOUR, 40 MINUTES

1 cup table salt

2 lb. Jerusalem artichokes

1⅓ lb. sweet onions

1 qt. white vinegar

3 cups sugar

1 Tbsp. dry mustard

¾ tsp. ground turmeric

¾ tsp. freshly ground black pepper

1 Tbsp. mustard seed

¼ tsp. ground allspice

1. In a 1-gallon container, combine salt with ½ gallon water. Stir until salt is nearly all dissolved.

2. Wash and scrub Jerusalem artichokes well; pat dry. Peel and chop into small pieces. (You should have 5 cups.) Cut onions into fourths. Slice thinly. (You should have 5 cups.) Add artichokes and onions to salt mixture. Cover, chill, and soak overnight. Drain in a colander, using a large spoon to press out extra liquid.

3. Bring vinegar and sugar to a boil, uncovered, in a Dutch oven. Boil 15 minutes.

4. Combine mustard and remaining ingredients. Toss vegetables and dry ingredients together; add to vinegar mixture. Return to a boil. Remove from heat.

5. Fill and process jars as described on page 139. Store properly sealed jars in a cool, dark place. Let stand at least 3 days for the best flavor before serving.

GROWING YOUR OWN HERBS

For the price of one bunch of herbs at the grocery store, you can purchase one plant at a garden store and harvest your own herbs all season long. I love the convenience of walking a few steps outside my kitchen to snip basil or thyme. Even for those who weren't born with a gardening gene, herbs are possible, even easy. They are low-maintenance plants that require little attention and are forgiving with watering amounts. They thrive in pots. A sunny windowsill, patio, tiny balcony, or sprawling yard all work for herbs to flourish. These plants are a good way to start gardening and begin enjoying the fresh flavors they add to recipes.

Try planting mint in a pot and then planting the entire pot in the ground. It will keep the roots from spreading and taking over any other spots it can find. Rosemary and oregano prefer a little drier soil than their more water-loving cousins of sage, basil, and parsley. Thyme is nice to grow as a creeping groundcover. The best thing about any herb is the more you clip it, the more it grows.

Mushrooms

Mushrooms grow by absorbing moisture in the air. Thanks to Southern humidity, there's no shortage here. Mushrooms are like sponges, so it's best not to submerge them in water. They will only soak up water if you do. You can rinse them lightly if they are very dirty, but then pat them dry immediately and use right away. The best way to remove soil is simply to wipe off each mushroom with a dry kitchen towel.

There are several varieties that are available in most markets. Cremini, a young portobello mushroom, is similar in size to a standard button mushroom but has much more flavor. The spongy, honeycomb-like morels are fairly easy to find dried, but if you come across fresh ones at a farmers' market, buy them. Each bite is a treat. Shiitakes have flat tops with a dense texture and inedible stems. Porcinis have a slight toasted nut flavor. Wood ears are nice for adding variety to a combination of mushrooms thanks to their lack of stems and flat, flexible shape. Chanterelles are the Cadillac of mushrooms and are sometimes sold at farmers' markets. From summer and early fall, the golden orange frills excite those lucky enough to find them.

Choose ones that are free of mold and have no soft spots or bruises. Store them in a paper bag or on a tray covered with paper towels in the refrigerator. Mushrooms are happiest when air can circulate around them.

WILD MUSHROOM SOUP

This soup shows the range mushrooms, from fresh to dried, have to offer.

MAKES 6 SERVINGS   HANDS-ON 25 MINUTES   TOTAL 1 HOUR, 30 MINUTES

1 (0.5-oz.) package dried porcini
   mushrooms
1 (0.5-oz.) package dried morel
   mushrooms
1 (0.5-oz.) package dried
   chanterelle mushrooms
¾ cup Madeira wine*
3¾ cups chicken broth, divided
¼ cup butter
6 green onions, sliced
1 medium onion, diced
3 Tbsp. all-purpose flour
1 (8-oz.) package fresh
   mushrooms, quartered
¼ tsp. black pepper

1. Chop dried mushrooms. Bring mushrooms, wine, and ½ cup chicken broth to a boil in a small saucepan. Remove from heat, and let stand 30 minutes.

2. Melt butter in a large saucepan or Dutch oven over medium-high heat; add green onions and diced onion; sauté until tender.

3. Stir in flour, and cook, stirring constantly, 5 minutes. Gradually stir in remaining 3¼ cups chicken broth. Stir in wine-hydrated mushroom mixture, fresh mushrooms, and pepper; bring to a boil. Reduce heat, and simmer, uncovered, stirring occasionally, 30 minutes.

*Use chicken broth instead of Madeira wine, if desired.

CREAMY MUSHROOM GRITS

MAKES 6 SERVINGS   HANDS-ON 20 MINUTES   TOTAL 20 MINUTES

2 (3.5-oz.) packages shiitake
   mushrooms
¼ cup butter
1 cup quick-cooking yellow grits
½ cup grated Parmesan cheese
1 tsp. kosher salt
½ tsp. black pepper
¼ cup chopped fresh parsley

1. Stem and slice mushrooms. Melt butter in a medium skillet over medium-high heat; add mushrooms. Sauté 3 to 4 minutes or until mushrooms begin to brown.

2. Prepare grits according to package directions. Stir in cheese, kosher salt, and pepper. Stir in mushrooms and parsley.

ARTICHOKE-STUFFED MUSHROOMS

Stuffed mushrooms were a Southern cocktail party staple for years. The artichokes add a perfectly tangy taste to the hearty mushrooms. They are certainly worth revisiting again and bringing back the legend.

MAKES 25 TO 30 APPETIZERS   HANDS-ON 33 MINUTES   TOTAL 1 HOUR

1½ lb. large fresh mushrooms
¼ cup chopped onion
2 garlic cloves, chopped
1 Tbsp. olive oil
¼ cup dry white wine
¼ cup soft breadcrumbs
1 (14-oz.) can artichoke hearts,
    drained and chopped
3 green onions, chopped
½ cup grated Parmesan cheese
½ cup mayonnaise
¼ tsp. table salt
¼ tsp. freshly ground black
    pepper
Garnish: fresh thyme leaves

1. Preheat oven to 350°F. Rinse and pat mushrooms dry. Remove stems, and chop; reserve mushroom caps. Sauté mushroom stems, onion, and garlic in hot oil in a large skillet over medium heat 5 minutes or until onion is tender.

2. Add wine, and cook 2 minutes or until liquid evaporates. Stir in breadcrumbs. Remove from heat, and let cool.

3. Combine onion mixture, artichoke, and next 5 ingredients. Spoon 1 teaspoon into each mushroom cap. Place on a lightly greased rack in a roasting pan.

4. Bake at 350°F for 12 to 15 minutes or until golden.

sage advice

Once bread is too stale to enjoy, make fresh breadcrumbs. Simply pulse the dry bread in a food processor, and store in the freezer for up to three months.

COMPANY POT ROAST WITH CREAMY MUSHROOM GRITS

With very little work, a slow cooker makes this supper worthy of company. Swapping out standard rice or mashed potatoes with dressed-up grits is a very Southern upgrade.

MAKES 6 SERVINGS**HANDS-ON 40 MINUTES****TOTAL 9 HOURS, INCLUDING GRITS**

6 medium leeks, root end and dark green tops removed
4 thick bacon slices
1 (4- to 4½-lb.) boneless chuck roast, trimmed
2 tsp. freshly ground black pepper
1½ tsp. kosher salt
2 Tbsp. olive oil
3 garlic cloves, minced
⅓ cup firmly packed light brown sugar
1 cup dry red wine
⅓ cup balsamic vinegar
1 lb. carrots, cut into 4-inch sticks
1 lb. parsnips, cut into 4-inch sticks
1 cup chicken broth
1 Tbsp. cornstarch
Creamy Mushroom Grits (page 183)
Garnish: fresh flat-leaf parsley

1. Cut a slit in leeks lengthwise, and rinse thoroughly under cold running water to remove grit and sand. Place leeks in a lightly greased 5- to 6-quart slow cooker.

2. Cook bacon in a large skillet over medium heat 6 to 8 minutes or until crisp. Remove bacon, and drain on paper towels, reserving 3 tablespoons hot drippings in skillet. Crumble bacon.

3. Sprinkle roast with pepper and salt. Add olive oil to hot drippings in skillet. Place roast in skillet, and cook over medium-high heat 2 to 3 minutes on each side or until browned. Transfer roast to slow cooker, reserving 1 tablespoon drippings in skillet.

4. Add garlic to hot drippings, and sauté 30 seconds. Add brown sugar, stirring until sugar melts. Add wine and balsamic vinegar, and cook 2 minutes, stirring to loosen browned bits from bottom of skillet. Pour mixture over roast, and top with carrots and parsnips.

5. Cover and cook on LOW 8 to 10 hours or until meat shreds easily with a fork. Transfer roast to a cutting board; cut into large chunks, removing any large pieces of fat. Transfer roast and vegetables to a platter, and keep warm.

6. Skim fat from juices in slow cooker, and transfer juices to a 2-quart saucepan. Add broth, and bring to a boil over medium-high heat. Stir together cornstarch and 2 tablespoons water in a small bowl until smooth; add to pan, stirring until blended. Boil 1 minute. Add salt and pepper to taste. Serve gravy with roast and vegetables over Creamy Mushroom Grits. Top with crumbled bacon.

Turnips

Depending on where you grew up in the South, some refer to turnips as the root and to others that means the greens. Try to buy turnips as a whole, with the greens still attached. The greens should be vibrant and dark green with firm roots. As a general rule, the smaller the turnip root, the more mild the flavor will be. Larger ones can lean towards spicy.

If needed, peel the larger ones and cut them into pieces before cooking. In old Southern kitchens, turnip greens used to be cooked for what seemed like forever. Now, we know shorter times work just as well. Store uncooked greens in a damp towel in the refrigerator.

FALL VEGETABLE HASH

Serve this filling side dish with a beef roast or roasted salmon. Make use of some frozen summer corn to add color and sweetness to this recipe. Try any of your favorite fall root vegetables in place of the turnips and sweet potatoes.

MAKES 8 SERVINGS   **HANDS-ON 35 MINUTES**   **TOTAL 35 MINUTES**

4 thick bacon slices

2 Tbsp. olive oil

1 medium-size sweet onion, chopped

1 medium-size sweet potato (about 10 oz.), peeled and cut into ½-inch cubes

2 medium turnips (about 12 oz.), peeled and cut into ½-inch cubes

1 Tbsp. white wine vinegar

1 lb. small fresh Brussels sprouts, quartered

2 garlic cloves, sliced

1. Cook bacon in a 12-inch cast-iron skillet over medium heat, turning occasionally, 8 to 10 minutes or until crisp. Remove bacon; drain, reserving 2 tablespoons drippings in skillet. Coarsely chop bacon.

2. Add oil to hot drippings in skillet. Cook onion and sweet potato in hot oil and drippings over medium heat, stirring occasionally, 5 minutes. Add turnips; cook, stirring occasionally, 8 minutes.

3. Combine vinegar and 2 tablespoons water. Add Brussels sprouts, garlic, and vinegar mixture to skillet. Cover and cook, stirring occasionally, 5 minutes or until vegetables are tender. Stir in bacon; add salt and pepper to taste.

sage advice

Choose a variety of fresh and cooked vegetables for the best vegetable plate. Having this diversity gives contrasts in warm and satisfying with crunchy texture and bright flavors. Chopped herbs and citrus segments add simple and fresh flavors. I love to include pickles, chutneys, and relishes for the acid to play off the rich vegetables.

—Peter Dale, chef at The National in Athens, GA

GRITS AND END-TO-END TURNIPS

Hakurei turnips are mild and white as snow. Common in farmers' markets, they often are an easy first step into the world of loving larger, more traditional turnips. As the weather starts to cool, a bowl of these grits will keep you warm and satisfied from the inside out. Make sure to taste the grits to see if they're done. It's the only way to tell.

MAKES 4 TO 6 SERVINGS   **HANDS-ON 1 HOUR, 35 MINUTES**   **TOTAL 1 HOUR, 35 MINUTES**

4 cups milk, divided
1 cup stone-ground grits
2 tsp. table salt, divided
1¾ lb. hakurei turnips
1½ Tbsp. olive oil
¼ tsp. freshly ground black pepper
1 garlic clove, minced
2 oz. Parmigiano-Reggiano cheese, freshly grated
1 Tbsp. unsalted butter

1. Combine 3 cups milk, 2 cups water, grits, and 1½ teaspoons salt in a small Dutch oven or 4-quart saucepan. Cook over medium heat, stirring often, 30 minutes. Add ½ cup milk. Continue to cook, stirring often, for 30 more minutes. Add 1 cup water. Cook about 25 more minutes or until grits are creamy and no longer crunchy.

2. Meanwhile, preheat oven to 400°F. Cut turnip roots from stems and cut into fourths. Toss with olive oil, remaining ½ teaspoon salt, and ¼ teaspoon pepper. Arrange on a baking sheet in a single layer, and roast at 400°F for 35 to 40 minutes, tossing once, or until browned and tender.

3. Stir garlic into grits. Slice turnip greens into ½-inch ribbons. Stir remaining ½ cup milk and greens into grits. Cook for 8 minutes, stirring often.

4. Add cheese and butter, and stir until melted. Serve roasted turnip roots on top of grits.

SOUTHERN TURNIP GREENS AND HAM HOCKS

If you grew up eating turnip greens and ham hocks, you'll recognize this recipe. Many a Southern night has been warmed by this comforting dish.

MAKES 8 TO 10 SERVINGS   HANDS-ON 32 MINUTES   TOTAL 2 HOURS, 47 MINUTES

1¾ lb. ham hocks, rinsed
2 bunches fresh turnip greens
   with roots (about 10 lb.)
1 Tbsp. sugar

1. Bring ham hocks and 2 quarts water to a boil in an 8-quart Dutch oven. Reduce heat, and simmer 1½ to 2 hours or until meat is tender.

2. Remove and discard stems and discolored spots from greens. Chop greens, and wash thoroughly; drain. Peel turnip roots, and cut in half.

3. Add greens, roots, and sugar to Dutch oven; bring to a boil. Reduce heat; cover and simmer 45 to 60 minutes or until greens and roots are tender.

✦ sage advice ✦

Ham hocks have long flavored Southern vegetables as they simmered on the stove. The smoked and cured meat adds flavor in a much more natural way than bouillon. Ham hocks are normally not sold in packs of less than two. Store any extra ham hocks tightly wrapped in the freezer for up to six months.

PRECIOUS HEIRLOOMS

Heirloom vegetable seeds are often passed from generation to generation. These seeds haven't been modified or altered to produce more attractive vegetables, more insect-tolerant plants, or longer shelf lives. They produce the very same vegetable as the seeds did 100 years ago, and the flavor is almost always better than the hybrids that are widely available today.

Starting heirloom vegetables from seed can be one saving grace in the middle of a cold winter when you're itching for the ground to thaw. I like starting with the Seed Savers Exchange or Monticello catalogs for seed shopping and information. Flipping through these beautiful catalogs, you'll be shocked at the number of varieties available for your favorite vegetables.

One benefit to planting heirloom seeds is that you can find the exact variety that grows well in your region and choose a seed based on the qualities you like in that particular vegetable like smaller squash or sweeter peppers. Local extension services are a fantastic resource for gardeners to learn details like the best times to plant.

Winter Squash

Native Americans had a long tradition of planting squash and pumpkins. Even centuries later, the hard-skinned squash remains a cool-weather staple. Harvested in fall, these squash often last well into winter when stored at room temperature in the dark.

When shopping, look for squash that are heavy for their size with no soft spots. The harder the squash, the better. There are just about as many varieties of winter squash as you can dare to cook. Buy only squash with the stems attached.

WINTER SQUASH LASAGNA

MAKES 6 TO 8 SERVINGS   HANDS-ON 40 MINUTES   TOTAL 1 HOUR, 43 MINUTES

2 (1½- to 2-lb.) butternut
    squash
2 (1-lb.) acorn squash
3 Tbsp. extra virgin olive oil
2 tsp. table salt, divided
¾ tsp. freshly ground black
    pepper, divided
1½ cups ricotta cheese
1 tsp. chopped fresh thyme
¼ tsp. freshly grated nutmeg
¼ cup unsalted butter
1 garlic clove, minced
1 tsp. chopped fresh sage
¼ cup all-purpose flour
3 cups milk
6 oz. Parmigiano-Reggiano
    cheese, freshly shredded,
    divided
2 oz. goat cheese
½ (16-oz.) package lasagna
    noodles
Garnishes: fresh thyme sprigs,
    ⅓ cup pine nuts, toasted

1. Preheat oven to 425°F. Cut butternut squash in half lengthwise. Use a spoon to scoop out seeds. Reserve seeds for another use (refer to toasting seeds on page 200). Cut halves into 2 pieces widthwise. Cut acorn squash in half (so that the stem end is on one half). Use a spoon to scoop out seeds. Reserve seeds for another use.

2. Place squash pieces, cut sides up, on a jelly-roll pan. Brush all cut sides with olive oil, and sprinkle with ½ teaspoon salt and ¼ teaspoon black pepper. Bake at 425°F for 1 hour or until fork-tender. The squash will be browned. Allow squash to cool to room temperature, about 30 minutes. Reduce oven temperature to 350°F.

3. Use a spoon to remove squash from the skins. Discard the skins. Mash cooked squash with a potato masher. Stir in ricotta, thyme, ½ teaspoon salt, ¼ teaspoon pepper, and nutmeg.

4. In a medium saucepan, melt butter over medium-low heat. Add garlic and sage, and cook 2 minutes, stirring constantly. Add flour, whisking constantly; cook 1 minute. Whisk in milk, and cook 15 minutes, whisking often, or until thickened. Remove from heat, and stir in 4 ounces Parmigiano-Reggiano, 2 ounces goat cheese, remaining 1 teaspoon salt, and ¼ teaspoon pepper. Cook lasagna noodles according to package directions. Drain.

5. In a lightly greased 13- x 9-inch baking dish, spread 1 cup cheese sauce. Top with a layer of 3 noodles, and then with 3¼ cups squash mixture. Top with 3 noodles, 1 cup cheese sauce, and 3¼ cups squash. Top with remaining noodles, remaining cheese sauce (about 1½ cups), and remaining (about ¾ cup) Parmigiano-Reggiano. Cover the dish with foil. Bake at 350°F for 45 minutes. Remove foil, and cook until lightly browned (about 10 minutes).

NOTE: To make ahead, assemble entire lasagna. Cover and refrigerate for up to 2 days. Let stand at room temperature 45 minutes before baking as directed.

SPICED BUTTERNUT-PUMPKIN SOUP

Fall isn't official at our house until a warm bowl of this soup arrives on our table. It includes all the season's flavors: apples, sweet potatoes, pumpkins, and butternut squash. A food processor or hand blender works just as well for blending the soup.

MAKES 15 CUPS   HANDS-ON 30 MINUTES   TOTAL 1 HOUR, 35 MINUTES

2 Tbsp. butter

1 large sweet onion, diced

1 large red bell pepper, chopped

3 garlic cloves, minced

2 Tbsp. finely grated fresh ginger

1 medium butternut squash, peeled and cubed (about 1¾ lb.)

1 small pumpkin, peeled and cubed (about 1¾ lb.)

1 large sweet potato, peeled and cubed

1 large Granny Smith apple, peeled and cubed

1 (32-oz.) container reduced-sodium chicken broth

2 bay leaves

1½ tsp. red curry paste*

½ tsp. freshly ground black pepper

¾ cup whipping cream

1 Tbsp. fresh lime juice

Garnish: fresh sage

1. Melt butter in a large Dutch oven over medium-high heat; add onion and bell pepper, and sauté 8 minutes or until onion is golden. Stir in garlic and ginger, and cook 1 minute. Add squash, next 7 ingredients, and 4 cups water. Bring to a boil, reduce heat to medium-low, and simmer 20 minutes or until vegetables are tender. Remove from heat, and let stand 30 minutes, stirring occasionally. Remove and discard bay leaves.

2. Process soup, in batches, in a blender until smooth. Return to Dutch oven, and stir in cream. Bring to a simmer over medium heat; stir in lime juice, and add salt and pepper to taste.

*1 teaspoon curry powder may be substituted.

NOTE: 3 pounds butternut squash may be substituted for 1¾ pounds butternut squash and 1¾ pounds pumpkin.

⋙ put 'em up ⋘

Roasting squash and pumpkin seeds is one way to use almost every part of the vegetable. Soak the seeds in salted water for 3 hours, and then rinse. If the fibers don't come clean with rinsing, repeat the soaking for one more hour. Dry the seeds, and toast at 300°F for 10 to 15 minutes. Try adding seasonings, such as salt, cinnamon, olive oil, or cumin, to vary the flavor.

ACORN SQUASH WITH PEAR STUFFING

Growing up, we always had acorn squash stuffed with applesauce. This is a much more sophisticated way to include sweet fruit with savory squash. The sweetened orange juice sauce is not to be missed.

MAKES 4 SERVINGS   HANDS-ON 39 MINUTES   TOTAL 1 HOUR, 39 MINUTES

2 acorn squash
2 Tbsp. butter
1 small onion, chopped
2 medium pears, peeled
   and chopped
2 Tbsp. light brown sugar
2 Tbsp. bourbon
1 tsp. table salt
½ tsp. ground ginger
½ tsp. ground nutmeg
1½ cups orange juice
¾ cup sugar
Garnish: orange zest

1. Preheat oven to 400°F. Cut ¼ inch off ends of each squash. Cut each squash in half lengthwise; remove and discard seeds and membranes. Place squash halves, cut side down, in a 13- x 9-inch baking dish. Add water to depth of 1 inch.

2. Bake, covered, at 400°F for 45 minutes. Drain. Return squash halves to dish, cut side up. Set aside. Reduce oven temperature to 350°F.

3. Melt butter in a large skillet over medium heat; add onion, and cook, stirring occasionally, 20 minutes. Add pear and next 5 ingredients; cook, stirring occasionally, 5 minutes. Spoon mixture into squash halves.

4. Bake at 350°F for 15 to 20 minutes.

5. Meanwhile, bring orange juice to boil in a small saucepan. Stir in sugar, and boil 10 minutes. Serve over squash.

sage advice

For my Thanksgiving decorations, I like to buy pretty winter squash to make long-lasting table centerpieces and arrangements on trays and platters. Choose a mixture of colors and shapes for the most appeal. Then, after the holiday, the decorations can be cooked and served as part of a meal.

Winter

There's no better time to warm up with dark leafy greens
and rich tubers than while the cold air is swirling outside.
It is these hardy stars of the shortest days of the year that often
get us through until the tender entrance of springtime.

Brussels Sprouts

Brussels sprouts were first grown in Louisiana thanks to French settlers. California became the first state to grow them on a large production scale, since the little sprouts tend to like cooler climates.

Look for smaller heads that are bright green and compact. Peel away very loose or bruised leaves, and remove the core before cooking. As a general rule, the shorter the cooking time on Brussels sprouts, the less of the signature smell arises. Roasting at a high temperature, frying, and shredding and sautéing are all excellent ways to brown them and highlight their best qualities.

Store in an open bag up to one week in the refrigerator.

CAST-IRON BLISTERED BRUSSELS SPROUTS

Erase your memories of boiled Brussels sprouts and fall in love with the star of winter. Once the little gems meet a smoking-hot pan, they become crispy and get finished with a crazy-good sauce.

MAKES 4 SERVINGS   HANDS-ON 15 MINUTES   TOTAL 15 MINUTES

1 lb. fresh Brussels sprouts
3 Tbsp. canola oil
¾ tsp. kosher salt
1 Tbsp. honey
1 Tbsp. hot water
1 Tbsp. minced garlic
    (about 2 cloves)
1 Tbsp. soy sauce
¼ tsp. dried crushed red
    pepper
½ cup torn fresh mint leaves

1. Heat a 12-inch cast-iron skillet over medium-high heat 5 minutes. Remove outer leaves and stems from Brussels sprouts, and cut in half lengthwise.

2. Add canola oil to skillet, and tilt skillet to evenly coat bottom. Place Brussels sprouts, cut sides down, in a single layer in skillet. Cook, without stirring, 4 minutes or until browned. Sprinkle with kosher salt; stir and cook 2 more minutes. Stir together honey and hot water. Stir garlic, soy sauce, dried crushed red pepper, and honey mixture into Brussels sprouts. Stir in mint leaves, and serve immediately.

sage advice

For light cleaning, rub the cast-iron skillet with kosher salt and wipe clean with a damp towel. If the pan needs a more thorough cleaning, scrub it with a little water and a stiff brush. Then heat the cleaned pan on top of the stove to thoroughly dry all the water. Use a kitchen towel to rub on a light coating of oil.

BRUSSELS SPROUTS AND BACON SALAD

Thinly slicing raw Brussels sprouts is the key to this hearty, crunchy salad. Try it as a side for a grilled steak or roasted chicken. If you have any extra dressing, it's a good dip for just about anything.

MAKES 4 TO 6 SERVINGS   HANDS-ON 23 MINUTES
TOTAL 50 MINUTES, INCLUDING DRESSING

6 oz. thick bacon, cut into
    ½-inch pieces (about 5 slices)
1 sweet onion
1 lb. fresh Brussels sprouts
Buttermilk Green Goddess
    Dressing

1. Cook bacon in large skillet over medium-low heat 15 minutes or until crispy. Using a slotted spoon, remove bacon, reserving drippings in skillet. Drain and set aside.

2. Cut onion in half. Slice halves into ¼-inch slices. Cook in hot drippings over medium-low heat for about 12 minutes, stirring often, or until lightly browned.

3. While onion cooks, remove outer leaves and stems from Brussels sprouts, and cut in half lengthwise; then cut into ¼-inch slices.

4. Toss together Brussels sprouts, onion, and desired amount of dressing. Sprinkle with bacon before serving. Serve immediately.

BUTTERMILK GREEN GODDESS DRESSING

MAKES ABOUT ¾ CUP   HANDS-ON 5 MINUTES   TOTAL 5 MINUTES

1 small garlic clove, peeled
2 anchovies, packed in oil
¼ cup chopped fresh flat-leaf
    parsley
2 Tbsp. chopped fresh chives
1 Tbsp. chopped fresh tarragon

1 Tbsp. fresh lemon juice
¼ cup buttermilk
⅓ cup mayonnaise
⅛ tsp. freshly ground black
    pepper

Pulse garlic and anchovies in a food processor until finely chopped. Add remaining ingredients, and process until smooth.

FRIED BRUSSELS SPROUTS WITH PEANUT VINAIGRETTE

I love starting a meal with friends over a family-style appetizer. It sets everyone at ease and is a nice way to get the conversation started. A platter of these crispy bites really shines alongside a cold beer or glass of Champagne.

MAKES 6 SERVINGS   HANDS-ON 17 MINUTES   TOTAL 31 MINUTES

¼ cup white wine vinegar

1 Tbsp. sorghum syrup

3 Tbsp. creamy peanut butter

1 tsp. chopped fresh chives

2 lb. Brussels sprouts

Canola oil

½ sweet onion, cut into ¼-inch strips

½ tsp. kosher salt

1 red chile pepper, thinly sliced

¼ cup chopped fresh flat-leaf parsley

1. Whisk together vinegar, sorghum, peanut butter, and chives until combined. Set aside.

2. Remove outer leaves and stems from Brussels sprouts, and cut in half lengthwise.

3. Pour oil to depth of 1½ inches in a Dutch oven. Heat over medium-high heat to 375°F. Set a wire rack over a rimmed baking sheet for draining. Fry Brussels sprouts, in two batches, for 4 minutes each, and onion, in one batch, for 2 minutes or until crispy and deep golden brown. Drain.

4. Arrange Brussels sprouts and onion on a platter. Sprinkle with salt. Drizzle with peanut butter vinaigrette. Top with pepper slices and parsley. Serve immediately.

Cabbage

Have fun exploring just which cabbages are your favorites. From red to wrinkled and crinkled Savoy, there is one that will stand out for you. Look for bright cabbages with no bruises or signs of neglect. Mixing a few varieties for recipes is also a fun way to showcase all this underappreciated vegetable has to offer. Just like with Brussels sprouts, the faster they cook, the less they smell.

Don't forget the core of the cabbage. Dice it and include it in dishes like slaw.

Store cabbage in the refrigerator in an open bag for up to four days.

BRAISED CABBAGE WITH APPLE AND BACON

Using red cabbage with tart apple slices and bacon elevates this common winter vegetable to a side dish fit for the holidays.

MAKES 6 TO 8 SERVINGS   HANDS-ON 35 MINUTES   TOTAL 1 HOUR, 20 MINUTES

4 thick bacon slices, cut into
  ¼-inch pieces
4 celery hearts, thinly sliced,
  leaves reserved
1 medium onion, thinly sliced
2 tsp. fennel seeds (optional)
½ cup dry white wine
1 head red cabbage (about
  2 lb.), thinly sliced
1 cup reduced-sodium fat-free
  chicken broth
1 cup unfiltered apple cider
1 garlic clove, thinly sliced
2 bay leaves
1 tart apple, thinly sliced
1 Tbsp. apple cider vinegar

1. Cook bacon in a Dutch oven over medium heat 4 minutes on each side or until crisp; remove bacon from pan, and drain. Reserve 3 tablespoons drippings in pan.

2. Increase heat to medium-high. Add celery, onion, and, if desired, fennel seeds, and sauté 6 minutes. Add wine, and cook 2 minutes or until reduced by half. Stir in cabbage and next 5 ingredients. Add salt and pepper to taste.

3. Reduce heat to low. Cover and cook 45 minutes or to desired tenderness. Stir in vinegar. Discard bay leaves. Top with celery leaves and bacon.

sage advice

Celery leaves are often overlooked and discarded, but they actually have more flavor than the stalks. Make good use of the instant flavor boost they can provide by adding them to salads and using them as garnish.

SOUTH CAROLINA SLAW

This is a refreshing change of pace from heavier, mayonnaise-based slaws. With two kinds of mustard and tangy apple cider vinegar, it's begging for a barbecue sandwich. If taking the slaw to a tailgate, add the dressing right before serving.

MAKES 6 CUPS   HANDS-ON 15 MINUTES   TOTAL 15 MINUTES

½ head thinly sliced cabbage
    (about 1 lb.)
1 cup shaved carrot
½ cup apple cider vinegar
¼ cup sugar
¼ cup vegetable oil
2 Tbsp. Dijon mustard
2 tsp. dry mustard
1 tsp. celery seeds
1 tsp. kosher salt
½ tsp. freshly ground black
    pepper

1. Place cabbage and carrot in a bowl.

2. Whisk together vinegar, sugar, vegetable oil, Dijon mustard, dry mustard, celery seeds, kosher salt, and pepper in a saucepan until sugar dissolves; bring to a boil over medium-high heat. Pour over cabbage mixture; toss to coat. Serve immediately.

KITCHEN COMPOSTING

For those stems, skins, and bruises that can't justify a place on the plate, try composting them to make sure that nothing goes to waste. With a simple combination of air, water, carbon-rich "browns" and nitrogen-rich "greens," those scraps that aren't usable in the kitchen can be a welcome addition in the garden.

Finding a compost bin that meets your needs for space, capacity, and ease of stirring is the place to start. Combine two-thirds "browns" like coffee grounds, tea bags, paper, and leaves with one-third "greens" like egg shells, fruit and vegetable peelings, and dead flowers, and sprinkle with water. The mixture should be damp, not soggy. You can add scraps to the bin as often as you like, but be sure to stir the compost at least once a week, and add water if it becomes dry. Not only does composting keep vegetable scraps out of the landfill, but it also recycles them into a nutrient-dense addition to the soil for next season's harvest.

Greens

Greens have been the mainstay of Southern meals for generations. In general, the smaller leaves are more desirable in all kinds of greens. Collards and chard are more tender and mustard leaves are less spicy when they are smaller. Avoid yellow or shriveled leaves. They all need to be washed very well before cooking. Swish them in water in a clean sink, the way you would hand-wash laundry (with no soap). Try sautéing the flowers or garnishing your next recipe with them. Store clean greens in a loose bag in the refrigerator for up to three days.

BACON-AND-BOURBON COLLARDS

Bourbon, bacon, and beer give collards a rich and earthy flavor. The vinegar added at the end gives a zip to a hearty cold-weather side dish.

MAKES 10 SERVINGS   HANDS-ON 40 MINUTES   TOTAL 1 HOUR, 40 MINUTES

4 thick bacon slices

3 Tbsp. butter

1 large sweet onion, diced

1 (12-oz.) bottle beer

½ cup firmly packed brown
   sugar

½ cup bourbon

1 tsp. dried crushed red pepper

6 lb. fresh collard greens,
   trimmed and chopped

½ cup apple cider vinegar

1 tsp. table salt

½ tsp. freshly ground black
   pepper

1. Cut bacon crosswise into ¼-inch strips. Melt butter in a large Dutch oven over medium heat; add bacon, and cook, stirring often, 8 minutes or until crisp. Drain bacon on paper towels, reserving drippings in skillet. Sauté onion in hot drippings 3 minutes or until onion is tender. Stir in bacon, beer, and next 3 ingredients; cook 3 minutes or until mixture is reduced by one-fourth.

2. Add collards, in batches, and cook, stirring occasionally, 5 minutes or until wilted. Reduce heat to medium-low; cover and cook 1 hour or to desired degree of doneness. Stir in vinegar, salt, and pepper.

sage advice

For boiling leafy greens...the greens should be fresh and crisp, with any stems broken off, leaving only the leaves. (Stalks can be tied into a bundle and used for stock.)
   —Edna Lewis in *The Taste of Country Cooking* (Knopf, 1976)

COLLARD-AND-OLIVE PESTO

When collards are in abundance, set some aside for this versatile pesto. The olives and lemon give a tangy punch to the famous Southern green.

MAKES 3 CUPS   HANDS-ON 20 MINUTES   TOTAL 20 MINUTES

1 cup pitted green olives

4 garlic cloves

1 lb. washed, trimmed, and chopped collard greens

1 tsp. lemon zest

2 Tbsp. fresh lemon juice

1 Tbsp. white wine vinegar

2 tsp. kosher salt

1 tsp. freshly ground black pepper

1 cup extra virgin olive oil

1 cup grated Parmesan cheese

1. Process olives and garlic in a food processor until finely chopped. Add collard greens, lemon zest, lemon juice, vinegar, salt, and pepper; pulse 6 to 8 times or until collards are finely chopped.

2. With processor running, pour olive oil through food chute in a slow, steady stream. Add cheese, and pulse until smooth. Keep refrigerated in an airtight container up to 3 days.

put 'em up

When the greens come in by the armful, make the most of each leaf with pesto. Freeze ¼-cup portions in zip-top plastic freezer bags. It's a dream for making a quick pasta sauce or adding to sandwiches or salad dressings. For additional recipes, see pages 36 and 239.

MUSTARD GREENS WITH YOGURT-PARMESAN DRESSING

Mustard greens can be spicy. This clever salad lets you decide how fiery you like the greens. For less spice, toss the salad with the dressing a few minutes before serving. Or if you're like me and like it spicy, add the dressing at the table. You'll be tempted to eat all the bacon croutons as soon as they come out of the oven.

MAKES 4 TO 6 SERVINGS   HANDS-ON 30 MINUTES   TOTAL 55 MINUTES

3 cups (1-inch) French bread
   baguette cubes
5 thick bacon slices
1 Tbsp. minced shallot
2 Tbsp. white wine vinegar
1 tsp. lemon zest
2 Tbsp. fresh lemon juice
1 cup Greek yogurt
2 Tbsp. extra virgin olive oil
½ cup (2 oz.) finely grated
   Parmigiano-Reggiano cheese
1 bunch mustard greens,
   washed, trimmed, and torn
½ tsp. kosher salt
¼ tsp. freshly ground black
   pepper

1. Preheat oven to 350°F. Arrange bread cubes in a single layer in a jelly-roll pan. Place bacon slices over bread cubes, so that most of bread is covered. Bake at 350°F for 25 to 30 minutes or until bacon and bread are crisp.

2. Meanwhile, stir together shallot and next 3 ingredients in a medium bowl. Let stand 10 minutes. Whisk in yogurt, oil, and grated cheese.

3. Crumble bacon; toss bacon and croutons with greens. Arrange salad on a platter. Drizzle 3 to 4 tablespoons dressing over salad. Sprinkle with salt and pepper. Serve immediately with remaining dressing.

sage advice

Serving hearty greens, like mustard, kale, and collards, raw in salads is a great way to keep weekly menus fresh and new while still getting in their valuable nutrition. Thanks to sturdy leaves, dressings hold very well on greens and the salads don't wilt as quickly as lettuce does.

OTTO WITH SWISS CHARD

...arely gets such a vitamin boost as it does when it's combined with ... ...ard. Using patience and adding the broth a little at a time will keep risotto creamy.

MAKES 8 SERVINGS   **HANDS-ON 43 MINUTES**   **TOTAL 43 MINUTES**

8 cups torn Swiss chard leaves (about 9 oz.)

4¾ cups vegetable broth

2 tsp. olive oil

½ cup finely chopped onion

1 cup uncooked Arborio rice or other short-grain rice

3 Tbsp. dry vermouth or dry white wine

⅛ tsp. ground nutmeg

3 Tbsp. grated Parmesan cheese

⅛ tsp. freshly ground black pepper

1. Combine chard leaves and ½ cup water in a large saucepan. Bring to a boil; cover, reduce heat, and simmer 10 to 15 minutes or until tender. Drain well, and set aside.

2. Bring broth to a simmer in a medium saucepan (do not boil). Keep warm over low heat.

3. Heat oil in a large saucepan over medium-high heat. Add onion; cook, stirring occasionally, 5 minutes or until tender. Add rice; sauté 1 minute. Add vermouth; sauté 30 seconds. Add warm broth, ½ cup at a time, stirring constantly until each portion of broth is absorbed before adding the next (about 25 minutes total). Add chard leaves, nutmeg, cheese, and pepper; cook, stirring constantly, 2 minutes or until thoroughly heated.

⤳ sage advice ⤳

Potlikker is the liquid that remains in the pot after greens are cooked. Save every drop and never throw out this vitamin-packed liquid gold. Try it with cornbread and savor an old Southern tradition.

Rutabagas

Most rutabagas have been coated with wax before selling to help seal in moisture. The wax must be peeled off with a vegetable peeler before cooking.

Peeling and slicing a rutabaga can be made easier by cutting a small slice off one side and resting it on the flat side. Hold the rutabaga with a kitchen towel to keep it steady while cutting it into several slices. It may take a rocking motion to get through the entire vegetable. Next, use a vegetable peeler to peel the slices. Peel thick slices off to get down to the meat. Look for firm rutabagas with a hue of purple on the top.

Some find rutabagas bitter. That can change from vegetable to vegetable, but if you do run across one that you find too bitter to enjoy, simply blanch it in salted water after peeling and it will neutralize the bitterness.

Store rutabagas in an open bag in the refrigerator for up to one week.

SMASHED RUTABAGAS AND TURNIPS WITH PARMESAN

Skip the mashed potatoes and try a combination of rutabagas and turnips instead. With Parmesan cheese, butter, and cream, they become rich and satisfying alongside a roasted turkey.

MAKES 6 SERVINGS   HANDS-ON 15 MINUTES   TOTAL 1 HOUR

1 lb. rutabagas, peeled and
   chopped
1 tsp. table salt
1½ lb. turnips, peeled and
   chopped
¼ cup grated Parmesan cheese
6 Tbsp. butter
½ cup whipping cream
¾ tsp. table salt
¼ tsp. freshly ground black
   pepper
2 Tbsp. bourbon (optional)

1. Combine rutabagas, 1 teaspoon salt, and 6 cups water in a large Dutch oven; bring to a boil, and cook 25 minutes. Add turnips, and cook 20 more minutes or until vegetables are tender; drain.

2. Combine vegetables, cheese, and next 4 ingredients in a large mixing bowl; mash with a potato masher (or beat at medium speed with an electric mixer) to desired consistency. Stir in bourbon, if desired.

POTATO-AND-RUTABAGA GRATIN

It would be difficult to find a prettier presentation of rutabaga than this gratin. Layered in a parchment paper-lined cast-iron skillet to bake to golden brown, it dazzles hungry guests as it's turned out onto a platter.

MAKES 8 SERVINGS   HANDS-ON 1 HOUR, 30 MINUTES
TOTAL 3 HOURS, 5 MINUTES

1 large rutabaga
4 medium-size red potatoes
¼ cup butter
¼ cup all-purpose flour
2 cups whipping cream
1 tsp. table salt
¼ tsp. ground white pepper
¼ tsp. ground red pepper
Dash of ground nutmeg
½ cup grated Parmesan cheese
Parchment paper
Garnishes: fresh sage,
    rosemary sprigs

1. Preheat oven to 400°F. Peel, quarter, and thinly slice rutabaga. Peel and thinly slice potatoes; set aside.

2. Melt butter in a heavy saucepan over low heat, and add flour, stirring until smooth. Cook, stirring constantly, 1 minute. Gradually add whipping cream, and cook over medium heat, stirring constantly, until mixture is thickened and bubbly. Stir in salt and next 3 ingredients. Set sauce aside.

3. Sprinkle cheese in a 10-inch cast-iron skillet lined with parchment paper or aluminum foil, and arrange half of rutabaga slices over cheese. Layer with ¾ cup sauce, potato slices, and ¾ cup sauce. Arrange remaining rutabaga slices on top, and add remaining sauce. Cover skillet tightly with aluminum foil.

4. Bake at 400°F for 1 hour; uncover and bake 20 more minutes. Let stand 15 minutes. Invert onto a serving platter. To serve, cut into wedges.

SAVVY SHOPPING WITH ORGANICS AND LOCALLY GROWN PRODUCE

Organic vegetables have been grown without pesticides, herbicides, and synthetic fertilizers. Many times shopping at farmers' markets is an easy way to find organic produce that's grown very near your hometown on small family farms.

When reading labels in stores, the term "local" is more difficult to define. It can mean in your county or it can mean in a bordering state. When in doubt, always ask someone from the grocery store. For the easiest, most personal way to find the very freshest, best vegetables possible, find a local farm or farmers' market and buy directly from those who grew what you'll cook. It's a system that usually makes everyone happy.

Spinach

Spinach has unfortunately been sold in bags for salads for so many years that buying a fresh bunch seems quite foreign these days. It's such a pleasure to choose a bunch of the green leaves from a farmers' market or pick them straight from your garden. The two different types of spinach are identified by the look of their leaves. The leaves are either flat or crinkled. The crinkled leaves are sturdier and hold dressing better than their flat cousins. The flat leaves are nice for wilting or creaming. Remove the stems and add them to stock for vegetable soup. The leaves should be bright green, full of life, and perky. Wilted leaves are not the ones you want.

Baby spinach is available everywhere as washed, bagged, and ready-to-go. The flavor on these immature small leaves is less than leaves that were allowed to grow to a larger size. They do not hold up as well to cooking but are preferred by many in salads.

Wash spinach leaves very well to remove any sandy soil. Remember that spinach cooks down drastically, when you're buying what seems like mounds and mounds of the bright green leaves. One pound of spinach cooks down to about 1 cup.

Store spinach in an open bag in the refrigerator for three to four days.

SAUSAGE, BEAN, AND SPINACH DIP

I like to call this a manly dip. It's the ultimate combination for those who want a dip that's more than just a little snack. Serve with corn chip scoops, bell pepper strips, and pretzel rods.

MAKES ABOUT 6 CUPS   HANDS-ON 25 MINUTES   TOTAL 45 MINUTES

1 sweet onion, diced
1 red bell pepper, diced
1 (1-lb.) package hot ground
    pork sausage
2 garlic cloves, minced
1 tsp. chopped fresh thyme
½ cup dry white wine
1 (8-oz.) package cream cheese,
    softened
6 oz. fresh baby spinach,
    coarsely chopped
¼ tsp. table salt
1 (15-oz.) can pinto beans,
    drained and rinsed
½ cup (2 oz.) shredded
    Parmesan cheese
Serve with: corn chip scoops,
    red bell pepper strips,
    pretzel rods

1. Preheat oven to 375°F. Cook diced onion, bell pepper, and sausage in a large skillet over medium-high heat, stirring often, 8 to 10 minutes or until meat crumbles and is no longer pink. Drain. Stir in garlic and thyme; cook 1 minute. Stir in wine; cook 2 minutes or until liquid has almost completely evaporated.

2. Add cream cheese, and cook, stirring constantly, 2 minutes or until cream cheese is melted. Stir in spinach and salt, and cook, stirring constantly, 2 minutes or until spinach is wilted. Gently stir in beans. Pour mixture into a 2-quart baking dish; sprinkle with cheese.

3. Bake at 375°F for 18 to 20 minutes or until golden brown.

sage advice

Save time and skip the step of removing stems from baby spinach. The leaves are so tender that they need no extra knife time at all.

SPINACH AND PECAN-STUFFED PORK CHOPS

A wimpy pork chop is a disappointment. This recipe uses a real-deal, meaty chop, with the surprise of flavorful spinach inside. Depending on appetites, one chop may feed more than one. Get your steak knife ready!

MAKES 4 TO 6 SERVINGS   **HANDS-ON 48 MINUTES**   **TOTAL 1 HOUR, 13 MINUTES**

5 oz. fresh spinach

¼ cup chopped pecans, toasted

½ cup Parmigiano-Reggiano cheese, grated on a box grater

2 Tbsp. panko (Japanese breadcrumbs)

1 garlic clove, grated

1 tsp. lemon zest

1 tsp. kosher salt, divided

½ tsp. freshly ground black pepper, divided

4 (12-oz.) bone-in pork chops

1 Tbsp. extra virgin olive oil

1. In a large nonstick skillet over medium heat, add spinach, and cover. Let steam for 2 to 3 minutes; remove cover, and stir until wilted and tender, about 1 more minute. Scrape into a fine wire-mesh strainer, and let cool. Squeeze out as much liquid as possible. Finely chop.

2. In a medium bowl, combine chopped spinach, pecans, cheese, breadcrumbs, garlic, lemon zest, and ½ teaspoon salt and ¼ teaspoon pepper. Set aside.

3. Use a paring knife to cut a large pocket in each pork chop. Starting on the side of the chop opposite the bone, cut into the chop until the tip of the knife touches the bone. The opening where the knife entered should be about 1 inch wide. Without widening the opening, fan the knife through the chop to create a pocket. Use your fingers to feel through the opening.

4. Preheat grill to 350° to 400°F (medium-high) heat. Using your fingers, stuff the pork chops each with ¼ cup of the filling, flattening the pork to make sure the filling has spread through the whole pocket. Pockets should be as filled as possible. Rub chops with olive oil on all sides, and season with remaining salt and freshly ground pepper.

5. Grill, without grill lid, 8 minutes per side, flipping once, or until stuffing registers 140°F. Allow to rest 10 minutes before serving.

VEGETABLE GNOCCHI WITH SPINACH PESTO

Baking the vegetables before stirring in with the gnocchi gives them just the right amount of texture. Look for gnocchi on the aisle with the dried pastas.

MAKES 4 SERVINGS   **HANDS-ON 10 MINUTES**   **TOTAL 45 MINUTES, INCLUDING PESTO**

6 yellow squash (about 1¼ lb.)
8 sweet mini bell peppers
2 Tbsp. olive oil
1 tsp. table salt
½ tsp. coarsely ground black
    pepper
1 (16-oz.) package gnocchi*
Spinach-Herb Pesto
3 oz. fresh baby spinach
¼ to ⅓ cup (1 to 1½ oz.) freshly
    shredded Parmesan cheese

1. Preheat oven to 425°F. Cut squash into 1-inch pieces. Cut bell peppers in half lengthwise; remove seeds. Stir together squash, bell peppers, oil, salt, and ground pepper. Arrange vegetables in a single layer on a jelly-roll pan, and bake at 425°F for 15 minutes. Stir and bake 5 more minutes or until tender and golden.

2. Cook gnocchi according to package directions in a Dutch oven; drain. Return to Dutch oven. Add Spinach-Herb Pesto to gnocchi, and toss to coat. Add squash mixture and spinach, and gently toss to combine. Sprinkle with cheese. Serve immediately.

*Medium-size pasta shells may be substituted.

SPINACH-HERB PESTO

MAKES ¾ CUP   **HANDS-ON 15 MINUTES**   **TOTAL 15 MINUTES**

3 oz. fresh baby spinach
1 Tbsp. chopped fresh cilantro
1 Tbsp. chopped fresh basil
1 tsp. lemon zest
2 Tbsp. fresh lemon juice
1 tsp. chopped fresh mint

1 garlic clove, minced
¼ tsp. table salt
½ cup (2 oz.) freshly shredded
    Parmesan cheese
¼ cup olive oil

Pulse first 8 ingredients in a food processor 6 or 7 times or until finely chopped. Add cheese and oil; process until smooth, stopping to scrape down sides as needed. Use immediately, or store in refrigerator up to 48 hours.

Sweet Potatoes

Sweet potatoes and yams have been on Southern tables for generations, and most who eat them can't describe the difference between the two or why they have two different names. A true yam is an entirely different vegetable and doesn't grow in North America. There are two types of sweet potatoes here. One has more moisture and soft flesh. The other is harder and has a dry flesh. Right or wrong, Southerners have taken to calling the moist, softer fleshed sweet potatoes yams. The moist-skinned potatoes usually have a deeper orange or even purplish skin.

Sweet potatoes are fairly fragile, much more so than other potatoes. Their skins are thin and they last only for a little over a week at room temperature. Don't wash them until right before you're ready to cook them.

ROASTED SWEET POTATOES WITH CRANBERRIES

It can't be the holidays at our house without the sound of cranberries popping in the kitchen. While in the oven, the rosemary crisps and the cranberries give up their tartness, one at a time. This dish is the epitome of winter.

MAKES 4 TO 6 SERVINGS   **HANDS-ON 11 MINUTES**   **TOTAL 56 MINUTES**

3½ lb. sweet potatoes, peeled

5 Tbsp. extra virgin olive oil, divided

1 tsp. table salt, divided

½ tsp. freshly ground black pepper

1½ cups fresh cranberries

20 (2-inch) sprigs fresh rosemary

2 garlic cloves, minced

1. Preheat oven to 425°F.

2. Cut potatoes into 1½-inch pieces. Toss potatoes with 3 tablespoons olive oil on a jelly-roll pan; sprinkle with ¾ teaspoon salt and pepper. Roast at 425°F for 35 minutes (do not stir during this time).

3. Toss cranberries, rosemary, garlic, remaining ¼ teaspoon salt, and remaining olive oil in a small bowl. Add to potatoes, and stir gently. Roast 10 more minutes.

SWEET POTATO CASSEROLE

Creamy, rich sweet potatoes are speckled with crunchy cornflakes, pecans, brown sugar, and marshmallows for the ideal Thanksgiving combination in each serving.

MAKES 6 TO 8 SERVINGS   HANDS-ON 20 MINUTES   TOTAL 2 HOURS, 50 MINUTES

4½ lb. sweet potatoes

1 cup granulated sugar

¼ cup milk

½ cup butter, softened

2 large eggs

1 tsp. vanilla extract

¼ tsp. table salt

1¼ cups cornflakes cereal, crushed

¼ cup chopped pecans

1 Tbsp. brown sugar

1 Tbsp. butter, melted

1½ cups miniature marshmallows

1. Preheat oven to 400°F. Bake sweet potatoes at 400°F for about 1 hour or until tender. Let cool to touch; peel and mash sweet potatoes. Reduce oven temperature to 350°F.

2. Beat mashed sweet potatoes, sugar, and next 5 ingredients at medium speed with an electric mixer until smooth. Spoon potato mixture into a greased 11- x 7-inch baking dish.

3. Combine cornflakes cereal, pecans, brown sugar, and melted butter in a small bowl. Sprinkle over casserole.

4. Bake at 350°F for 30 minutes. Remove from oven; let stand 10 minutes. Sprinkle with marshmallows, and bake 10 more minutes. Let stand 10 minutes before serving.

sage advice

Shop for sweet potatoes that are all about the same size to ensure that the baking time for each potato will be the same. This prevents having to leave larger potatoes in the oven longer than planned.

SWEET POTATO CORNBREAD

Adding sugar to cornbread may be a big debate, but not when the sweetness comes from a sweet potato. Thanks to a little pumpkin pie spice, a pat of butter is all it needs.

MAKES 6 SERVINGS   HANDS-ON 15 MINUTES   TOTAL 50 MINUTES

2 cups self-rising white
   cornmeal mix
3 Tbsp. sugar
¼ tsp. pumpkin pie spice
5 large eggs
2 cups mashed cooked sweet
   potatoes (about 1½ lb. sweet
   potatoes)
1 (8-oz.) container sour cream
½ cup butter, melted

1. Preheat oven to 425°F. Stir together cornmeal mix, sugar, and pumpkin pie spice in a large bowl; make a well in center of mixture. Whisk together eggs and next 3 ingredients; add to cornmeal mixture, stirring just until moistened. Spoon batter into a lightly greased 9-inch square pan.

2. Bake at 425°F for 35 minutes or until golden brown.

ROASTED SWEET
POTATOES WITH
CRANBERRIES,
PAGE 241

SWEET POTATO
CORNBREAD,
PAGE 243

SWEET POTATO
CASSEROLE, PAGE 242

FANCY SWEET POTATO PIE

Baked sweet potatoes and lemon are hidden under a meringue made with marshmallow crème for the epitome of Thanksgiving desserts.

MAKES 8 TO 10 SERVINGS   HANDS-ON 20 MINUTES   TOTAL 2 HOURS, 30 MINUTES

½ (14.1-oz.) package refrigerated piecrusts

Parchment paper

1 large egg yolk, lightly beaten

1 Tbsp. whipping cream

¼ cup butter, melted

1 cup sugar

¼ tsp. table salt

3 large eggs

3 cups lightly packed, mashed cooked sweet potatoes (about 2½ lb. sweet potatoes)

1 cup half-and-half

1 Tbsp. lemon zest

3 Tbsp. fresh lemon juice

¼ tsp. ground nutmeg

3 large egg whites

½ tsp. vanilla extract

⅛ tsp. table salt

¼ cup sugar

1 (7-oz.) jar marshmallow crème

1. Preheat oven to 425°F. Roll piecrust into a 13-inch circle on a lightly floured surface. Fit into a 9-inch pie plate; fold edges under, and crimp. Prick bottom and sides with a fork. Line piecrust with parchment paper; fill with pie weights or dried beans. Bake at 425°F for 9 minutes. Remove weights and parchment paper.

2. Whisk together egg yolk and cream; brush bottom and sides of crust with yolk mixture. Bake at 425°F for 6 to 8 more minutes or until crust is golden. Transfer to a wire rack, and cool. Reduce oven temperature to 350°F.

3. Stir together melted butter, 1 cup sugar, ¼ teaspoon salt, and 3 eggs in a large bowl until mixture is well blended. Add sweet potatoes and next 4 ingredients; stir until mixture is well blended. Pour sweet potato mixture into prepared piecrust. (Pie will be very full.)

4. Bake at 350°F for 50 to 55 minutes or until a knife inserted in center comes out clean, shielding with aluminum foil to prevent excessive browning. Transfer pie to a wire rack, and cool completely (about 1 hour).

5. Increase oven temperature to 400°F. Beat egg whites, vanilla, and ⅛ teaspoon salt at high speed with a heavy-duty electric stand mixer until foamy. Gradually add sugar, 1 tablespoon at a time, beating until stiff peaks form. Beat one-fourth of marshmallow crème into egg white mixture; repeat 3 times with remaining marshmallow crème, beating until smooth (about 1 minute). Spread over pie. Bake at 400°F for 6 to 7 minutes or until meringue is lightly browned.

NOTE: Pie can be made up to a day ahead. Prepare recipe as directed through Step 4; cover and chill up to 24 hours. Proceed as directed in Step 5.

METRIC EQUIVALENTS

The information in the following charts is provided to help cooks outside the United States successfully use the recipes in this book. All equivalents are approximate.

COOKING/OVEN TEMPERATURES

	Fahrenheit	Celsius	Gas Mark
Freeze Water	32° F	0° C	
Room Temp.	68° F	20° C	
Boil Water	212° F	100° C	
Bake	325° F	160° C	3
	350° F	180° C	4
	375° F	190° C	5
	400° F	200° C	6
	425° F	220° C	7
	450° F	230° C	8
Broil			Grill

LIQUID INGREDIENTS BY VOLUME

¼ tsp					=	1 ml	
½ tsp					=	2 ml	
1 tsp					=	5 ml	
3 tsp	=	1 Tbsp	=	½ fl oz	=	15 ml	
2 Tbsp	=	⅛ cup	=	1 fl oz	=	30 ml	
4 Tbsp	=	¼ cup	=	2 fl oz	=	60 ml	
5⅓ Tbsp	=	⅓ cup	=	3 fl oz	=	80 ml	
8 Tbsp	=	½ cup	=	4 fl oz	=	120 ml	
10⅔ Tbsp	=	⅔ cup	=	5 fl oz	=	160 ml	
12 Tbsp	=	¾ cup	=	6 fl oz	=	180 ml	
16 Tbsp	=	1 cup	=	8 fl oz	=	240 ml	
1 pt	=	2 cups	=	16 fl oz	=	480 ml	
1 qt	=	4 cups	=	32 fl oz	=	960 ml	
				33 fl oz	=	1000 ml	= 1 l

DRY INGREDIENTS BY WEIGHT

(To convert ounces to grams, multiply the number of ounces by 30.)

1 oz	=	¹⁄₁₆ lb	=	30 g
4 oz	=	¼ lb	=	120 g
8 oz	=	½ lb	=	240 g
12 oz	=	¾ lb	=	360 g
16 oz	=	1 lb	=	480 g

LENGTH

(To convert inches to centimeters, multiply the number of inches by 2.5.)

1 in				=	2.5 cm	
6 in	=	½ ft		=	15 cm	
12 in	=	1 ft		=	30 cm	
36 in	=	3 ft	=	1 yd	=	90 cm
40 in	=				100 cm	= 1 m

EQUIVALENTS FOR DIFFERENT TYPES OF INGREDIENTS

Standard Cup	Fine Powder (ex. flour)	Grain (ex. rice)	Granular (ex. sugar)	Liquid Solids (ex. butter)	Liquid (ex. milk)
1	140 g	150 g	190 g	200 g	240 ml
¾	105 g	113 g	143 g	150 g	180 ml
⅔	93 g	100 g	125 g	133 g	160 ml
½	70 g	75 g	95 g	100 g	120 ml
⅓	47 g	50 g	63 g	67 g	80 ml
¼	35 g	38 g	48 g	50 g	60 ml
⅛	18 g	19 g	24 g	25 g	30 ml

INDEX

ABOUT THE AUTHOR

Rebecca Lang is an author, cooking instructor, television personality, and a ninth-generation Southerner. Born and raised in South Georgia, she is the author of six cookbooks, including *Fried Chicken, Around the Southern Table*, and *Quick-Fix Southern*.

Rebecca has a culinary arts degree from Johnson & Wales University and a journalism degree from the University of Georgia. She has appeared on *Fox & Friends Weekend*, multiple segments on QVC, WGN America's Midday News, and numerous regional and local networks. Rebecca and her cooking have been featured in more than 50 nationally televised *Southern Living* food segments and in publications such as *The Wall Street Journal, The Atlanta Journal-Constitution, The Washington Post*, the *Houston Chronicle, Wine Enthusiast,* FoxNews.com, *The Daily Meal,* and *Glamour* and *Fitness* magazines.

She serves as a contributing editor for *Southern Living,* teaches cooking classes across America, and writes a blog that has been featured on the James Beard Foundation blog, Delights and Prejudices, and noted in *Food News Journal*'s "Best of the Blogs." Rebecca is a cooking expert for Ty Pennington's website and writes a monthly recipe post. Her writing has appeared in many publications including *Southern Living, Disney's Family Fun, Taste of the South, The Atlanta Journal-Constitution, Flavors* magazine, and *Edible Atlanta.*

Rebecca lives in Athens, GA., with her husband, Kevin, and their children, Camden and Adair.

ACKNOWLEDGMENTS

I first learned the beauty and value of fresh vegetables from the women I loved the most. My mom, Mandy Dopson, and my grandmothers, Sarah Dopson and Claudia Thomas, set a fine example of putting up by the bushel. Our screened porch was often the best place to learn what was in season.

My husband, Kevin, and my children, Camden and Adair, are the world's best cheering section and recipe tasters. I am grateful for their patience with my sometimes-crazy schedule and menus that only recipe testers can get away with. Thanks to my parents, Mandy and William Dopson, I am able to do what I do. They gave me all the best building blocks for real life and now have become two talented babysitters.

My sister, Natalie Schweers, is nearly a one-woman PR firm. She turned me on to Jerusalem artichoke relish (thanks to Susan Barrett) and kept up with my vegetable adventures. Linda Lang, my mother-in-law, rivals Amazon in book sales.

My agent, Carole Bidnick, supported this book from the first mention to the last period. She's always behind me every step of the way.

Ivy Odom came on board with me as an intern and quickly became a colleague and good friend. She was a constant professional and was instrumental in making things happen.

Working with Oxmoor House is like coming home again. My editor, Rachel West, makes working on a book as smooth, pleasant, and fun as an author can ever ask for. It was a wonderful partnership. Maribeth Jones made each page worthy of a dream. I'm so grateful for the talent of Iain Bagwell, Victor Protasio, and Hélène Dujardin. The photography is stunning. For others at Oxmoor House who put in time and energy: Anja Schmidt, Katherine Cobbs, Felicity Keane, Melissa Brown, Lauren Moriarty, Melissa Clark, Kay Clarke, Mindi Shapiro, Catherine Steele, Victoria Cox, Margaret Dickey, Rishon Hanners, Nathan Carrabba, Alyson Haynes, Julia Levy, Karen Rankin, Callie Nash, Kellie Lindsey, Donna Baldone, Julie Bosché, Julie Gillis, Sue Chodakiewicz, and Diane Keener.

Nathalie Dupree ushered my career into existence and has held my hand through the years. Virginia Willis fills countless roles including friend, colleague, and therapist. I can't imagine a professional life without Mary Moore and her team at The Cook's Warehouse in Atlanta. Mark Kelly keeps me laughing at every phone call. No matter what I ask, Damon Fowler has the answer.

Lauren Cox and her team at Woodland Garden's in Athens, Georgia, helped keep me in fine, local produce. Robert Schueller at Melissa's Produce made recipe testing out of season possible. The quality and array of produce from Melissa's is nothing short of amazing.

Chef Michele Weaver generously shared vegetable insights. Chef Peter Dale paved the road to testing ramps and enlightened me on the best vegetable plate in the world.

Crystal Leach cheerfully read over my text before a deadline while in the passenger seat of my car after a long day of work. Georgiana Sumner loaned me a copy of *Charleston Receipts* when I was in desperate need.

Donna Means and Joseph Nunn made sure my hair was magical before the shutter ever clicked. Dr. and Mrs. Cobbs graciously opened their garden to us for photos. Celine Russell glamorously transformed me each morning before photography.

It indeed does take a village, and this one is a talented, strong, and very much Southern community.